Advice and Consent

t

Advice and Consent
The Politics of Judicial Appointments

Lee Epstein and Jeffrey A. Segal

OXFORD
UNIVERSITY PRESS

2005

OXFORD
UNIVERSITY PRESS

Oxford University Press, Inc., publishes works that
further Oxford University's objective of excellence
in research, scholarship, and education.

Oxford New York
Auckland Cape Town Dar es Salaam Hong Kong Karachi
Kuala Lumpur Madrid Melbourne Mexico City Nairobi
New Delhi Shanghai Taipei Toronto

With offices in
Argentina Austria Brazil Chile Czech Republic France Greece
Guatemala Hungary Italy Japan Poland Portugal Singapore
South Korea Switzerland Thailand Turkey Ukraine Vietnam

Copyright © 2005 by Oxford University Press, Inc.

Published by Oxford University Press, Inc.
198 Madison Avenue, New York, NY 10016
www.oup.com

Oxford is a registered trademark of Oxford University Press

Library of Congress Cataloging-in-Publication Data
Epstein, Lee, 1958–
Advice and consent : the politics of judicial appointments / Lee Epstein and Jeffrey A. Segal.
p. cm.
Includes bibliographical references and index.
ISBN-13: 978-0-19-530021-5
ISBN-10: 0-19-530021-1
1. Judges—Selection and appointment—United States.
I. Segal, Jeffrey Allan.
II. Title.
KF8776.E67 2005   347.73'14—dc22   2005018318

9 8 7 6 5 4 3 2 1
Printed in the United States of America
on acid free paper

To Nancy

L. EPSTEIN

To Christine

J. SEGAL

Acknowledgments

"We could not have written this book without the help of . . ." is the customary, if not perfunctory, first sentence of most acknowledgements. In our case, it's true. We could not have written this book without the help of Dedi Felman. Both of us have worked with excellent editors, but none has taken a greater interest nor loomed as large a presence in our writings than Dedi. If we worked day and night to put the final touches on this book—and there were days and nights that we did—so did Dedi. If we couldn't see the forest for the trees—and often we couldn't—Dedi saw both. She labored over every sentence, figure, and chapter with an eye toward ensuring the integrity of our work but at the same time making it accessible—no small feat when dealing with two academics. Not even these words can express our gratitude.

We feel much the same about all the other people with whom we worked at Oxford: Sue Warga, our copy editor; Betsy DeJesu, in public relations; Michele Bove, the master of photographs; and Catherine Humphries, who oversaw production. Each is just great at her job.

We wrote this book with overriding objective of making the seemingly arcane process of appointing federal judges more transparent to the public and students, but we couldn't have written it without the help of our colleagues in the academic community. Before we even set pen to paper, Dedi secured advice from James Pffifner, Sarah Binder, Mark Graber, David Yalof, Sheldon Goldman, and Lawrence Baum. Without their counsel, this book would have headed in a very different (mis)direction. We also gratefully acknowledge support from five members of our discipline who are always there for us, no questions asked: Gregory Caldeira, Micheal Giles, Walter F. Murphy, Harold J. Spaeth, and Thomas G. Walker. They will see traces of our many conversations and e-mail exchanges throughout.

Then there are our colleagues who, by virtue of their sheer generosity, don't realize the extent of their contribution. Topping the list is Sheldon Goldman. Not only did he lend a hand in the book's development, he also supplied information crucial to its completion. Without his data on judicial appointees, each chapter would have been weaker. Shelly's book Picking Federal Judges (Yale University Press, 1997) too served as an inspiration. Since the 1980s, Harold J. Spaeth has labored to produce his U.S. Supreme Court Database, which the New York Times reporter Linda Greenhouse once deemed a "computerized treasure trove." Not only do we agree, but we also admit here and now that we couldn't have written Chapter 5 without it. Public databases produced by Donald Songer and Wendy Martinek also contributed to our effort. Ryan Black and Christina Boyd, two ace Ph.D. students at Washington University, provided on-the-spot research assistance. We are indebted to them.

We also thank our families, and dedicate this book to the member in each who most patiently (though not always silently) endured our preoccupation (okay, obsession) with the politics of judicial appointments.

Finally, we ought note that as the book was going to press, President Bush nominated Judge John G. Roberts to the Supreme Court. While we did not know that Judge Roberts would get the nod, his name appears several times in our discussion of nominations (Chapter 3) and confirmations (Chapter 4).

L.E.—St. Louis, Missouri

J.A.S.—Stony Brook, New York

Contents

Advice and Consent

Introduction

Official portrait of Justice Louis D. Brandeis.
*Eben F. Comins, Collection of the Supreme
Court of the United States*

*When the president announced his nominee for the Supreme
Court, pandemonium broke out in the legal and political com-
munities, where many powerful elements had long fought and
feared the nominee. The* Wall Street Journal *declared, "In all
the . . . agitation of the past years one name stands out con-
spicuous above all others. Where others were radical, he was
rabid; where others were extreme, he was super-extreme." The
opposition was directed not only at the nominee's social and
economic record but also at his social background. The* New
York Sun *feared that this unqualified nominee might be approved only due to "the racial issue." Among the large number
of well-known opponents were distinguished members of the
organized bar, a former president of the NAACP, and the president of Harvard University. The confirmation battle raged
against a background of some of the ugliest charges ever lev-
eled against a distinguished servant. A former president even
referred to him as "an insidious devil."*[1]

Who was the nominee? Thurgood Marshall? Robert Bork? Clarence Thomas? Perhaps William H. Rehnquist? No. This story is about Louis Brandeis, whom President Woodrow Wilson nominated to the Supreme Court in 1916.

If this account of the Brandeis nomination indicates anything, it is that political clashes over candidates for the Supreme Court are not a new phenomenon. Quite the opposite. The appointment of justices is now and always has been a contentious process—one driven largely by partisan and ideological concerns.

Who supports which candidate has never been unrelated to the supporter's own party affiliation. It is probably no coincidence that Democratic senators were responsible for forty-six of the forty-eight votes against the Republican Clarence Thomas, or that Republicans cast all nine votes opposing the Democrat Stephen Breyer. In both instances, partisan concerns were at least partially at work.

Just as frequently ideology plays a role in the process's outcome. In fact, ideology, liberal or conservative, often trumps mere partisanship. Conservative Democrats did not let party loyalty stand in their way when they crossed the aisle and joined Republicans to block President Lyndon Johnson's appointment of the liberal Abe Fortas to the post of chief justice in 1968. Two decades later, when six of the Senate's most liberal Republicans voted against *their* president's nominee to the Supreme Court, the conservative Robert H. Bork, it was Ronald Reagan's turn to be abandoned by members of his own party.[2] In both cases, senators were willing to risk alienating their party to oppose candidates whose political preferences were incompatible with theirs and their constituents'.

We can say much the same about appointments at lower levels of the federal judiciary. While battles over nominees to the U.S. circuit courts are now more public and the outcomes less certain, it would be a mistake to conclude that politics, in the form of ideology and partisanship, plays a far greater role in the 2000s than it did in, say, the 1930s. When Franklin D. Roosevelt was president, senators expected to have some role in selecting his judicial nominees. When they felt inadequately consulted, they occasionally extracted revenge, whether by blocking the appointment or by foiling other presidential initiatives, just as contemporary senators do now.

This is not to say that features of the appointments process, and important features at that, have remained constant over time: nominees to the lower courts now garner scrutiny once reserved for candidates to the Supreme Court, and interest groups and the media are paying even more attention to Supreme Court nominees. But what has not changed is that, almost without exception, presidents from the early years of the United States to the present day have sought to exploit vacancies on the bench for ideological and partisan purposes. Senators have done much the same, supporting or opposing nominees who help further their own goals, primarily those that serve to advance their chances of reelection, their political party, or their policy interests. This was as true of John Adams and the Senate of 1800, which attempted to pack the courts with Federalists in order to advance their own interests, as it is now of George W. Bush and the Republicans in 2005, who desire a federal bench replete with conservatives.

Why politics, in the form of partisanship and ideology, plays such an extensive role in judicial appointments is not too difficult to understand. Presidents, senators, and interest groups alike realize that the judges themselves are political. Candidates for the federal bench receive their nominations precisely because through their political work or interests they came to the attention of some politician, most likely a U.S. senator or a member of the president's staff. Judges retain these partisan and ideological attachments when they ascend to the bench. When Socrates was on trial for his life, he may have refused to appeal to the "emotions" of judges out of the belief that the judge "has sworn that he will judge according to the laws and not according to his own good pleasure."[3] But the late great political scientist C. Herman Pritchett was far closer to the mark when he wrote that judges "are influenced by their own biases and philosophies, which to a large degree predetermine the position they will take on a given question. Private attitudes, in other words, become public law."[4]

That is why senators and presidents care so deeply about who sits on the federal bench—and so should we. If the decisions of federal judges reflected only the law or other "neutral" principles, then neither senators nor presidents would be able to fulfill their policy goals through appointments. But, as Pritchett so astutely observed, this "principled approach" does not always or even usually hold. In fact, with scattered exceptions here and there, the decisions of judges, and especially the decisions of Supreme Court justices, tend to reflect their own political values. More indirectly, these decisions also reflect the judges' partisan affiliation, which just so happens to coincide often with that of their appointing president.

John Adams believed in a strong national government, as did his choice for chief justice, John Marshall. Richard Nixon desired judges with a strong law-and-order posture and found one in Warren E. Burger, to say nothing of William H. Rehnquist.

We realize that this argument—namely, that the appointments process is and always has been political because federal judges and justices themselves are political—will trouble some commentators. There are those who will take issue with the first part of our argument, maintaining that the process has in fact changed markedly over the last two decades, and not for the better. These commentators have gone so far as to deem judicial confirmation proceedings a "mess," "abysmal," "badly broken," and downright "disorderly, contentious, and unpredictable."[5] To the extent that such characterizations reflect the growing presence of interest groups and the media, or the increasingly elevated and public battles over lower court nominees, we do not disagree. But we do indeed dispute the idea of an escalating reliance on ideology and partisanship on the part of senators and presidents; we do not believe wholesale change has occurred in this respect.

Then there are those who will challenge the second part of our argument. They will assert, even in the face of an extraordinary accumulation of evidence to the contrary, that "correct" answers to legal questions exist and that Socrates by and large got it right: judges are essentially neutral, with politics playing only a minor role. After all, the argument sometimes goes, by providing federal judges with life tenure rather than subjecting them to periodic public checks through the electoral process, the American constitution guarantees an independent (read apolitical) judiciary.

We hope to convince you otherwise. Our general plan is to begin at the beginning, with some background notes on the appointment process. We look at the formal constitutional rules that presumably govern the process and the informal rules that have developed over time and which actually define it. Next we explore the vacancies that presidents and senators are trying to fill. While the U.S. Constitution implies that the process of appointing judges begins with the president, it in fact starts with a vacancy on an existing court or, in some instances, a new seat. Both types of opening have been the subject of considerable commentary and debate, largely because political forces may play a role in generating the vacancy. In Chapters 3 and 4 we turn to the two stages of the appointments process: the nomination and confirmation of judges and justices. For each we explore the roles played by key actors—the president and his advisors, U.S. senators, and organized interests—as well as the factors they consider when making their choices to appoint or support particular nominees. Chapter 5 considers the outcomes of the process, the judges and justices themselves, and investigates the extent to which presidents (and senators) can shape judicial decisions through their nominees. We end with some thoughts on the implications of our analysis for the future of the appointments process. In light of Justice Sandra Day O'Connor's decision to leave the Supreme Court, Chief Justice Rehnquist's rumored retirement, and other vacancies that may well arise in the not-so-distant future, not to mention the rather stormy climate that characterizes contemporary American politics, the future is hardly a minor matter.

One final point is worth making here and now. Our focus on both judges and justices is no accident. While some books on the appointment process—and excellent volumes at that—focus exclusively on candidates for the U.S. Supreme Court, we take a broader approach, exploring nominees to all federal courts: district courts, circuit courts, and of course the high court.[6] This approach reflects the fact that contemporary debates over judicial appointments have centered on the nation's lower courts. That emphasis could be a consequence of any number of factors: growing interest group attention to these nominations, the lack of vacancies on the Supreme Court in recent years, the increasing tendency of presidents to select high court justices from the circuits, violations of long-standing norms on the part of contemporary senators (and presidents), or simply the growing importance of the courts of appeals. Which has mattered more, we do not know. What does seem clear is that the federal appellate courts, and to a lesser extent trial courts, deserve consideration. But we hardly ignore the U.S. Supreme Court. In fact, as you will soon see, we draw many of our substantive examples from nominations to this Court, which without doubt is the focal point of the U.S. judiciary.

1

A Backdrop
to Judicial
Appointments

Official portrait of Justice William O.
Douglas. *Elek Kanareck, Collection of the
Supreme Court of the United States*

Of all the difficult choices confronting societies when they go about designing their legal systems, among the most controversial are those pertaining to judicial selection and retention. How ought a nation select its judges and for how long ought those jurists serve?

These questions hardly escaped attention at America's constitutional convention in Philadelphia in 1787. The delegates had little difficulty reaching consensus on how federal judges ought to be tenured. After almost no debate they agreed that the new nation ought to follow British practice, which provided that federal judges should hold their "Offices during good Behaviour." Short of some form of malfeasance, judges would be retained for life.[1] This benchmark of "good Behaviour" might be less exacting than the "high crimes and misdemeanors" criterion the framers established for impeaching the president, but it was sufficiently rigorous to prevent removals for partisan or ideological concerns. The Senate, for example, refused to remove Justice Samuel Chase (served 1796–1811) simply because the Jeffersonians "wanted offices" occupied by their political opponents. Likewise, the House declined to rid the Supreme Court of William O. Douglas (served 1939–1975) for "moral turpitude" related to his serial marriages and publications in radical and obscene magazines.

On the other hand, over three months—virtually the duration of the entire convention—elapsed before the Philadelphia delegates reached an agreement over how federal judges should be selected. Delegates such as George Mason, Elbridge Gerry, and Oliver Ellsworth, who opposed a strong executive, wanted to follow the dominant state practice of the day and vest appointing authority in Congress. Others, such as Alexander Hamilton, James Madison, and Gouverneur Morris, wanted the executive to appoint judges.[2] A compromise finally resolved the matter by granting appointment power to the president, but only with the advice and consent of the Senate.[3]

Why rules governing the appointment of judges generated such controversy at the American constitutional convention and continue to prompt debate is an interesting question, with no shortage of answers. But surely a principal one is that politicians and the public alike believe that how we choose our judges plays a part in determining which types of men and women will serve as judges and, in turn, the choices that they will make in their post. For example, commentators of all ideological stripes agree that providing judges with life tenure usually leads to a more independent judiciary, one that places itself above the fray of ordinary politics. There is also agreement that subjecting judges to periodic checks conducted by the public or its elected officials, such as reelection or reappointment, may lead to more accountable courts. Where commentators diverge is over how the balance between independence and accountability should be struck. While some argue for lifetime appointments to induce independence, others hold that accountability requires a threat of enforcement, including the possibility of removal by the people or their representatives (see Figure 1.1). Taking the accountability argument to heart, only three U.S. states bestow life tenure on their judges.[4] In all others, judges must appear on the ballot to remain in office, though constitutional provisions vary from one state to the next. By the American Bar Association's tally, 80 percent of all state judges face election at some point in their career.

Understanding why the framers of the Constitution gave the president power to appoint yet made the confirmation conditional on Senate approval is a question that merits brief discussion. Only part of the story of judicial appointments in the United States lies in the arrangements described in the Constitution. Those arrangements are but a sketch, and over

Figure 1.1
Judicial Tenure and Appointment Practices Worldwide

Many societies elsewhere have eschewed the U.S. Constitution's approach of guaranteeing a lifetime appointment to their justices, opting instead for fixed terms of office. In South Africa, for instance, constitutional court justices hold office for a single twelve-year term; in Italy they are limited to a single nine-year term. In still others, including the Czech and Korean Republics, justices serve for a set, though renewable, term—a scheme usually designed to encourage accountability, perhaps to the point of subservience, among judges.

Moreover, constitutional framers elsewhere have made very different choices with regard to how justices are selected. In Germany, for example, the two houses of the Reichstag have the authority to choose the country's constitutional court justices, though six of the sixteen must be selected from among professional judges. In Bulgaria, one-third of the justices are selected by the parliament, one-third by the president, and one-third by judges sitting on other courts.

And yet these formal constitutional rules have their limits. While Germany's constitution states that the two houses of the Reichstag will choose the nation's constitutional court judges, in fact the process of appointment is a good deal more complicated than that simple provision suggests. Because election to the court requires support from a two-thirds majority, the two major political parties could in effect veto each other's candidates. To avoid such gridlock, an informal system of dividing up the seats has developed, such that half the seats belong to one party and half to the other. The result is a constitutional court that is relatively balanced between the interests of Germany's two major parties. But the process itself, including the informal division of seats on the Court, appears nowhere in the nation's constitution.

Source: Georg Vanberg, *The Politics of Constitutional Review in Germany* (2005).

time a number of informal procedures have developed to flesh out the process. It is only by understanding these informal norms that we can piece together the real story of how appointments to the federal bench work.

The Federal Judiciary

Perhaps because the majority of delegates to the Philadelphia Convention (thirty-four of fifty-five, to be precise) were lawyers or had some training in the law, or perhaps because they had observed legal systems at work both in the states and in England, many held a common vision of the general role courts would play in the new polity. Alexander Hamilton most famously expressed this view in "Federalist No. 78," one of a series of essays designed to garner support for the ratification of the Constitution. He envisioned a federal judiciary that would stand above the fray of ordinary politics, interpreting the Constitution and statutes free from overt partisan or ideological influence. To realize this vision and to prevent judges from evolving into legislators, the framers agreed on the need for judicial independence. They sought to instantiate this principle by providing judges with life tenure rather than subjecting them to popular election or renewal by Congress and by prohibiting legislators from punishing judges through salary reductions.

That the framers shared a fundamental commitment to an independent federal judiciary helped resolve some questions about how to design the federal legal system, such as whether judges should receive life tenure. But that commitment did little to lessen controversy over other matters, chiefly how to organize the courts and how to select the judges who would serve on them.

Structure of the American Legal System

A core issue before the delegates was how to structure the new judicial system. They had several choices: allow the states to retain the legal systems they had developed prior to 1787, eradicate state systems in favor of a national judiciary, or create a new federal system that would coexist with those in the states. In the end, they chose the third option but left their work somewhat incomplete.

Article III of the Constitution draws a blueprint for a federal court system but establishes only the Supreme Court. The question of whether to create federal tribunals inferior to the Supreme Court so divided the delegates that they ultimately left it up to the new Congress to work out. Some feared that federal courts would encroach on the power of state judiciaries. Others felt that lower federal tribunals were important to the creation of a strong national government. Deferral seemed the best option. In the words of Article III, "the judicial Power of the United States, shall be vested in one supreme Court, and in such inferior Courts as the Congress may from time to time ordain and establish."

The majority of founders anticipated that federal legislators would take up this invitation, and they were not wrong. The new Congress, full of supporters of a strong central government, quickly enacted the Judiciary Act of 1789. Still the most significant statute on the federal courts, the law was a defining moment in American legal history. It established the first system of federal courts, providing for a six-member Supreme Court, thirteen district courts, and three circuit courts.[5] Each of the eleven states that had ratified the Constitution received a district court, with separate tribunals created for Maine and Kentucky, which were then parts of Massachusetts and Virginia, respectively. District courts, then as now, were presided over by one judge and were grouped geographically into eastern, middle, and southern "circuits." Staffing each circuit was a district judge and two justices of the Supreme Court, who "rode circuit," that is, went around the circuit, usually on horseback or in a buggy, hearing cases. Under the Act of 1789 both the district courts and the circuit courts were trial courts, with the former hearing cases involving admiralty issues, forfeitures and penalties, petty federal crimes, and minor U.S. civil cases. Circuit courts had jurisdiction over cases involving citizens from different states and major federal criminal and civil cases.

Though the Act of 1789 continues to stand as a landmark, features of the U.S. judicial system have changed with time. Importantly, the circuit courts, now officially called U.S. Courts of Appeals, are no longer trial courts. Rather, as we show in Figure 1.2, they constitute the second level of what is a three-tiered judicial hierarchy, with cases flowing up from the district courts to the courts of appeals and then to the Supreme Court.[6] (Figures 1.3 through 1.5 provide information about each of these courts.) Thus, someone who is convicted in a district court has two levels of appeal.

Take Charles Katz, whom the FBI suspected of placing illegal gambling bets by telephone from Los Angeles to Miami and Boston in the mid-1960s. To gather evidence against Katz, FBI agents, without obtaining a warrant, placed listening devices outside the telephone booth he used to place his bets. The U.S. government then used the transcripts of those conversations to indict him. Because Katz violated a federal law, he would be tried in a federal court, and if he was convicted, he would have two shots at appeal: the federal appeals courts and the U.S. Supreme Court.

Figure 1.2
The Flow of Litigation in the Federal Judicial System, 2005

The Supreme Court

Litigants can ask the U.S. Supreme Court to review decisions of the U.S. Court of Appeals and, under certain instances, of state courts. Typically, those requests come in the form of petitions for a writ of certiorari, meaning that litigants ask the justices to become informed about their disputes by requesting the lower court to send up the record. It is up to the justices to decide whether to grant this request or not, and typically they do not. Of the eight thousand or so cases coming to the Court each year, the justices agree to decide, with a written opinion, only about eighty. Denial of certiorari does not necessarily mean that the Court agrees with the decision issued by the lower court; it simply means that, for whatever reasons, four justices did not find that the case merited the Court's scarcest resource, time. In general the Court accepts only cases that present substantial issues of law or that caused divisions among the lower courts.

U.S. Courts of Appeals

Litigants dissatisfied with the decision of a district court may appeal to the court of appeals located within their district. In civil cases either party may appeal. In criminal cases defendants may appeal if they are found guilty but the government may not appeal a verdict of not guilty. Both can appeal a sentence rendered after a guilty verdict. Persons dissatisfied with decisions made by certain federal agencies may also ask a court of appeals to review the agency's decision.

U.S. District Courts

As it turned out, Katz took advantage of both. Because he was arrested in Los Angeles his trial took place in a federal (U.S.) district court in California. Though Katz could have opted for a jury, he waived this right, preferring instead to have the judge decide his case. After that court convicted him, Katz appealed to the U.S. Court of Appeals for the Ninth Circuit. His petition asked the judges to reverse his conviction on several grounds, though most consequential was his assertion that the trial court should not have allowed the government to introduce transcripts from a "constitutionally protected area"—the phone booth—without a warrant.

Figure 1.3
The U.S. Supreme Court

There is one U.S. Supreme Court, on which eight associate justices and one chief justice serve. All nine justices hear and decide cases, which come primarily from lower federal courts and state courts. Once the Supreme Court agrees to decide a case, the parties present written and oral arguments to the Court, as they do in the circuits. After the justices review the briefs and hear arguments, they meet in a private conference to discuss the case and to take a preliminary vote. The conference typically leads to a tentative outcome and vote. That tentative vote, in turn, determines who assigns the writing of the opinion of the Court—the Court's authoritative policy statement, the only one that establishes precedent. Under Court norms, the chief justice assigns the writing of the opinion when he votes with the majority. The chief may decide to write the opinion or assign it to one of the other justices who voted with the majority. When the chief justice votes with the minority, the assignment task falls to the most senior member of the Court who voted with the majority. Whoever is assigned the opinion begins the process by circulating a draft to the other justices. They are free to join that opinion, "bargain" with the opinion writer, or circulate opinions of their own in the form of dissents or concurrences. Dissents are opinions that disagree with the outcome reached in the majority opinion (i.e., if the majority wants to affirm the decision of the lower court, the dissenters typically want to reverse it) and usually with the reasoning invoked in the majority opinion. Concurring opinions, on the other hand, typically agree with the outcome but may take issue with the reasoning or simply wish to make a different point than the majority. Eventually, the final version of the opinion is reached, and each justice expresses a position in writing or by signing an opinion of another justice. This is how the final vote is taken. When all of the justices have declared themselves, the only remaining step is for the Court to announce its decision and the vote to the public.

But Katz fared no better with this court. The three-judge panel unanimously affirmed his conviction.

That left Katz with the sole option of an appeal to the apex of the American legal system, the U.S. Supreme Court. His prospects for convincing the justices to take his case seemed bleak. In 1967, the year he requested review, the Court agreed to hear only about 250 of the 3,000 cases it received. But Katz was one of the lucky ones. Not only did the Court decide

Figure 1.4
U.S. Courts of Appeals

The ninety-four U.S. judicial districts are organized into twelve regional circuits, each of which has a United States Court of Appeals, known until 1948 as circuit courts of appeals. Eleven of the circuits are numbered (e.g., the Fifth Circuit covers the states of Louisiana, Mississippi, and Texas; in the Tenth are Colorado, Kansas, New Mexico, Oklahoma, Utah, and Wyoming); the twelfth court of appeals sits in the District of Columbia and is known as the U.S. Court of Appeals for the District of Columbia. In addition to these regional circuits, the U.S. Court of Appeals for the Federal Circuit has nationwide jurisdiction to hear appeals in certain kinds of disputes—primarily those involving patent laws and cases decided by the Court of International Trade and the Court of Federal Claims. Between six and twenty-eight judges staff each circuit. Usually they sit in panels of three to hear cases, though if a circuit decides to review the decision of a panel, the judges may sit en banc, that is, all together (or mostly all together in the case of some of the larger circuits). Appellate courts do not hear from witnesses or examine additional evidence; rather, they make decisions based on the existing record of the trial court or agency. In some instances they make decisions based exclusively on written briefs filed by attorneys; in others they hear oral arguments from the litigants' attorneys. Either way, the appealing party (the appellant) attempts to convince the judges that the trial court or administrative agency made an error in its decision; the appellee defends the decision previously issued. If the judges decide to hear oral arguments, they typically allot each side fifteen to thirty minutes to present its case, though they are free to interrupt the attorneys with questions. The decisions of courts of appeals usually will be the final word in the case—unless, of course, they return the case to the tribunal below for additional proceedings or the litigants appeal to the Supreme Court. But the probability of the Court agreeing to hear their dispute is quite low—about 1 percent.

to hear his case, it also found in his favor. When Katz entered the phone booth, he expected privacy. And as Justice Harlan wrote in his concurring opinion in the now landmark decision that is *Katz v. United States*, "that expectation [is] one that society is prepared to recognize as 'reasonable.'"[7] By invading that privacy without obtaining a warrant, the FBI violated Katz's constitutional rights.

Figure 1.5
U.S. District Courts

The U.S. district courts are the nation's trial courts for almost all cases in the federal system—about 260,000 civil and 60,000 criminal cases per year. There are ninety-four district courts—at least one in each state, and one in the District of Columbia and Puerto Rico—staffed by about 680 judges. Each of the ninety-four judicial districts also includes a U.S. Bankruptcy Court. U.S. district courts are courts of general jurisdiction, that is, they have authority to hear and decide most types of federal criminal and civil cases. The Court of International Trade and the Court of Federal Claims are special trial courts that have jurisdiction over only certain kinds of cases. The former hears cases on international trade and customs issues; the latter resolves disputes involving various claims against the United States, such as those over federal contracts and takings of private property by the federal government.

Katz's journey through the federal judicial system, while illustrative of the rare occasions on which an individual is able to take a case all the way to the Supreme Court, also masks the system's many complexities. One complication is that while the courts of appeals typically hear cases already decided by the district courts and the Supreme Court resolves disputes already heard in the courts of appeals, cases can also originate in the two top levels. Litigants, for example, may challenge the decisions of some federal agencies directly in the circuits, thus bypassing the district courts. If, say, a company wants to dispute an environmental rule established by the Environmental Protection Agency, it can do so in a court of appeals. It need not start in a trial court.

Likewise, the Constitution gives the Supreme Court original jurisdiction over certain kinds of cases. Original jurisdiction, when parties bring cases directly to the Supreme Court, applies in disputes in which a state is a party and those affecting ambassadors, public ministers, and consuls. Generally, however, the Court does not accept a suit invoking its original jurisdiction unless the justices believe there is a compelling reason of public policy. All the remaining business of the Supreme Court comes to it through its appellate jurisdiction, meaning that another court already has heard the case, as in the *Katz* example. The Court exercises this appellate jurisdiction according to the Constitution, "with such Exceptions, and under

such Regulations as the Congress shall make." In the post–Civil War period, Congress used this "exceptions clause" to prevent the justices from
reaching a decision in *Ex parte McCardle* (1869)—a decision that might
have been embarrassing to the Radical Republican Congress.

In *McCardle* the Supreme Court agreed that such action was within
congressional authority, though circumstances surrounding its decision
were exceptional enough as to make it hazardous to generalize from this
single ruling. So whether it would be constitutionally permissible for Congress to remove the Court's jurisdiction to decide, say, abortion or same-
sex marriage cases remains an open question. Until such litigation occurs,
Chief Justice Chase probably summed up the situation best when he noted,
after *McCardle* had been decided, that use of the exceptions clause was
"unusual and hardly to be justified except upon some impervious public
exigency."[8]

A second complexity in the American legal system is the existence of
state courts. By failing to eradicate the state courts operating at the time
that they wrote the Constitution, the framers contributed to the development of America's system of judicial federalism. Thus two complete systems of courts exist side by side in America, as each state has its own
judicial system, and to the extent that most are three-tiered, they resemble
the federal court hierarchy.[9] Moreover, the two systems really do coexist,
each ruling on disputes falling under its particular purview. If, for example,
the two authors of this book hijacked an airplane, we would be guilty of
violating a federal law and would be processed through the federal system. If, on the other hand, we stole a neighbor's car, we would be guilty of
violating a state law and would be processed accordingly through the state
system. As a general rule, federal courts resolve disputes implicating the
federal government, federal laws, the Constitution, or two or more states,
while state courts handle all matters of law in their jurisdictions, whether
civil or criminal in nature.

But that does not mean that state courts never hear claims made under
the U.S. Constitution or that federal courts necessarily shun cases litigated
in state courts. This was a lesson the nation learned all too well from the
now (in)famous case of *Bush v. Gore*. In that dispute, arising out of the 2000
presidential election, the Supreme Court's five most conservative justices
(Anthony Kennedy, Sandra Day O'Connor, William H. Rehnquist, Antonin

Scalia, and Clarence Thomas) blocked a decision of the Florida Supreme Court, which had ordered, in response to a suit filed by Vice President Al Gore, manual recounts in all counties in the state where "undervotes" had not already been recounted by hand. The Florida court's decision, the justices believed, ran afoul of the U.S. Constitution's equal protection clause because it failed to provide the guidance necessary to conduct the recounts.

By reversing the Florida court, the five justices handed the state's electoral votes, and thus a majority of the Electoral College, to Governor George W. Bush. So it seemed that the Supreme Court of the United States, or, more pointedly, its five most conservative members, all Republicans themselves, effectively decided the election of 2000 in favor of the Republican candidate.

Judicial Appointments

Among other lessons of *Bush v. Gore,* it is clear that when it comes to questions implicating federal law, it is the U.S. Supreme Court, not state courts, that has the final say. But the main lesson, and the one that has garnered far more attention, is that who serves on the federal courts matters, and matters a lot. Had five liberals (Democrats) sat on the Supreme Court instead of five conservatives (Republicans), we might have found ourselves writing about Al Gore's nominee to replace one of those Republicans, not about George W. Bush's candidate.

This basic point about the fundamental importance of a court's membership rarely escapes constitutional designers, and the framers of the U.S. Constitution were no exception. While questions over the structure of the judiciary were the cause of some controversy, including the fact that some delegates were opposed to creating any lower federal courts, the matter of how to select federal judges may have been even more vexing. At one point discussions were so heated that Benjamin Franklin proposed that lawyers should decide who should sit on the courts. The lawyers, Franklin joked, would select "the ablest of the profession in order to get rid of him, and share his practice among themselves."[10]

The delegates never took up Franklin's proposal. It was, by all accounts, an attempt at "entertainment." But they did consider at least seven others:

- All judges appointed by the legislature (both houses)
- All judges appointed by the executive

- Supreme Court justices appointed by the Senate, lower court judges appointed by both houses of the legislature
- All judges appointed by the Senate
- All judges nominated by the executive, "by and with the Advice and Consent" of the legislature
- All judges appointed by the executive unless two-thirds of the legislature disagreed
- All judges appointed by the Senate with the approval of (or veto by) the executive

Even after extensive debates over many of these proposals, but particularly over the larger consideration of whether to lodge the appointment power in the executive or the legislature, the framers found themselves so divided that they referred the matter to a special committee. Ironically enough, when that committee arrived at the arrangement that appears in the Constitution, nomination by the president with the advice and consent of the Senate, the delegates unanimously assented, even though they had deadlocked over a similar proposal offered by Alexander Hamilton less than two months earlier.

The Framers' Intent

The president "shall nominate, and by and with the Advice and Consent of the Senate, shall appoint" federal judges is precisely what the framers wrote, but what did they intend those words to mean?[11] Even today, in 2005, scholars and other commentators debate the answer, with at least two issues in serious contention.

The first centers on the balance of power between the Senate and the president. Some commentators contend the founders envisioned the Senate acting as only a "minor" check on the president. According to this argument, the appointment power is located in Article II, on the president, and not Article I, on Congress, precisely because the framers intended to give the president the edge. Alexander Hamilton, in *Federalist No. 76*, staked out this position when he asked what the Senate might do with presidential nominees:

> But might not his nomination be overruled? I grant it might, yet this could only be to make place for another nomination by himself. The person ultimately appointed must be the object of his preference, though perhaps not

in the first degree. It is also not very probable that his nomination would often be overruled. The Senate could not be tempted, by the preference they might feel to another, to reject the one proposed; because they could not assure themselves, that the person they might wish would be brought forward by a second or by any subsequent nomination. They could not even be certain, that a future nomination would present a candidate in any degree more acceptable to them.

To Hamilton, Senate confirmation would be a "silent operation," one that might prevent the president from nominating truly "unfit characters" but would not be a serious check on his authority.

Many presidents have concurred with this sentiment. John Adams once wrote that appointments were an "executive matter" that should be left to "the management of the executive." Richard Nixon, that great aggrandizer of presidential powers, also agreed that the appointment power was a "prerogative" of the executive. When the Senate was on the verge of defeating one of his nominees to the Supreme Court, Nixon declared that the Constitution entrusts "one person . . . with the power of appointment." The president's judgment should not be "frustrated by those who wish to substitute their own philosophy [for his]," Nixon continued. He falsely claimed that he was being denied "the same right of choice that has been freely accorded to my predecessors."[12]

Senators of Nixon's day strongly refuted this position, and joining them now are many legal scholars. That the framers endorsed the idea of "advice and consent," these scholars argue, suggests that it is the Senate's right, and indeed responsibility, to reject a president's nominees. That the Senate of 1795 exercised that right and rejected one of George Washington's Supreme Court nominees provides even stronger evidence that the founders never intended for the Senate to serve merely as a rubber stamp for the president.

The second and related debate over the framers' intent highlights the role of politics, partisanship, and ideology in judicial appointments. Here the controversy is less cut-and-dried, with at least three camps at odds. One group, forcefully represented by the well-known political scientist Henry Abraham, takes the position that the "delegates simply assumed, perhaps a mote naïvely, albeit quite understandably, that those selected as federal jurists would be chosen on the basis of merit. Period."[13] On this account, then, neither the president nor the Senate ought to consider a candidate's partisanship, philosophy, or ideology when they make their decisions; only ethics, competence, and integrity should play a role. A second set of commentators asserts that Abraham has it only half right: while the founders may have believed that "ideology—at least ideology . . . unrelated to a candidate's ability to fulfill his oath of office—simply had no place in the Senate's decision," they fully expected politics to play a role in the president's decision.[14] Yet a third camp takes issue with any account suggesting that the framers sought to remove ideology and politics from confirmation proceedings. To these commentators, the founders well understood the implications of the system they had devised. It was one that would invite the Senate, and of course the president, not just to scrutinize a candidate's professional qualifications but to examine, in ways that might also be political, the candidate's political values as well.

The Realities of the Appointments Process

We could go on and supply far more information about these controversies. Additional details, though, would serve only to highlight a rather simple point: that debates over the meaning of "advice and consent," like most debates over the intent of the framers—as if a single intent could ever exist for fifty-five people—will never be resolved. Or at least never resolved in the sense that we will ever know precisely what the framers intended.

On the other hand, time and practice have, in fact, resolved two points of contention. Both the president and the Senate play crucial roles in the process, and both incorporate politics into their calculus.

The Balance of Power Between the Senate and the President

"Advice and consent" is indisputably a vague term that could admit of a number of interpretations—and has, as we noted above. But the fact is, from the nation's earliest days the Senate has read those words to mean, at the very least, that it must approve presidential nominees by a majority vote.

That the Senate has taken this role seriously is beyond doubt. It has failed to confirm 27 of the 147 nominees to the Supreme Court over the past two centuries, rejecting the nominee outright in 12 of those cases (the other 15 were withdrawn, postponed, or not acted upon). During that same period, the Senate voted against a grand total of 9 nominations to the president's cabinet, 4 during President Tyler's administration alone. Likewise, from the start of Jimmy Carter's presidency in 1977 through the end of George W. Bush's first term in 2004, senators have not approved about 20 percent (69) of the 350 nominees to the U.S. Courts of Appeals and over 10 percent (131) of the 1,248 nominees to the U.S. District Courts.[15]

Certainly these figures hint at the degree of discretion exercised by the Senate over judicial appointments, but they may well be just the tip of the iceberg. First of all, owing to the very existence of the "advice and consent" clause, the president must take into account the preferences of senators when he makes a nomination or else risk the possibility of watching his nominee go down to defeat. Seen in this way, the Senate's power in the process may be far greater than simple counts of rejections suggest. After all, if the president attends to the interests of senators when deciding whom to nominate, then those senators would have no reason to reject his candidates. This is in part what Hamilton meant by the "silent operation" of the Senate's confirmation power. And it may explain, among other things, the Republican Gerald Ford's nomination, in the face of an overwhelmingly Democratic Senate, of the moderate John Paul Stevens rather than the more conservative Robert Bork to replace William O. Douglas in 1975.

But there is more. While it is clear that the Senate plays a crucial role in Supreme Court appointments (if only by constraining the president to choose among confirmable candidates), custom imposes tighter limitations on presidential freedom of choice for judges of the lower courts, especially the district courts. Indeed, as one senator once said, "It is a fact, though sometimes deplored by political scientists, that judges of the lower federal courts are actually 'nominated' by Senators while the President exercises nothing more than a veto authority."[16]

To see why, first consider what happens when any vacancy on the federal bench arises. As Figure 1.6 shows, the process typically begins in the executive branch. The president's advisors, including members of the Justice Department, compile lists of candidates and put together files. The names come from many sources, including state and federal politicians and other officials, interest groups, bar associations, and even the president. Candidates surviving this initial screening receive questionnaires about their personal lives, which they return to the Department of Justice. Traditionally, those surveys also went to the American Bar Association's

Standing Committee on Federal Judiciary, which the Department of Justice asked to evaluate the candidate informally. If the ABA committee's recommendation was favorable, the FBI ran a security check and the ABA committee was asked to issue a formal report (which included the votes of its members). But in 2001 President George W. Bush unilaterally ended, as is his prerogative, the ABA committee's semi-official role in conducting pre-nomination evaluations of judicial candidates. Bush advisors say that the president's decision was only a matter of equity. It is unfair, they claim, to allow one particular organization to play such a prominent role in recruiting judges when many other groups desire to participate. Outsiders, though, speculate that the decision can be traced back to the Reagan years, when ABA committee members split over Judge Robert H. Bork's fitness for service on the Supreme Court. That vote angered some Republicans then and continued to be a sticking point until the Bush administration cut the ABA loose.

With the FBI's report and other political and background information in hand, the president might make the final decision. Usually, however, one or more of his advisors makes the selection for vacancies on lower courts. The White House then transmits the nomination to the Senate, which in turn refers the matter to its Committee on the Judiciary. After hearings at which the candidate and other interested parties may testify, the Senate committee takes a vote. If the vote is favorable, the committee sends the nomination to the full Senate with a formal recommendation to confirm the candidate. Finally, the Senate votes. Nominees receiving the approval of a majority are then sworn in as federal judges.

This description of the appointments process is done in broad strokes. In practice, it is far more nuanced, especially with regard to the role of senators. When it comes to the Supreme Court, for example, senators do not expect to have much of a say in the first step in this process, that is, the nomination of justices. As a result, the president has wide discretion in naming any candidate he so desires, subject to the non-trivial constraint of Senate confirmation. At the district court level, though, senators expect to play a far more important and perhaps decisive role at the nomination stage. When a vacancy occurs on a district court, a senator from the president's party from that state will normally submit one or more names of candidates to the president's staff for consideration.[17] The president's advisors also may conduct their own search for promising talent, of course.

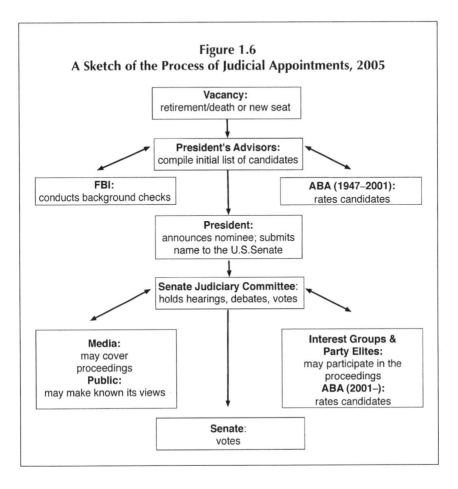

Figure 1.6
A Sketch of the Process of Judicial Appointments, 2005

But if there is a conflict of views between the senator and the administration, the senator can threaten to block confirmation by invoking the norm of senatorial courtesy. The Senate, following this norm, will only rarely confirm a nominee opposed by one or both home-state senators of the president's party.

The Senate shows the same courtesy over appointments to the courts of appeals. Even though the circuits cover more than one state, meaning that senators from several states can lay claim to a single appointment, it is generally the case that judgeships have been allocated by custom among the component states. Consequently, when a vacancy occurs, a senator frequently asserts that the successor should be from the same state as the former incumbent, thus giving the senator from that state a lien on the position. Senator Jesse Helms (R-N.C.) was for years able to prevent Bill Clinton from making an appointment to the Fourth Circuit (which covers North Carolina, along with South Carolina, Virginia, and West Virginia). The position, as we explain in more detail in Chapter 2, remained vacant until the end of 2000, when Clinton granted his candidate, Roger Gregory, a recess appointment. In a recess appointment, the president makes a unilateral appointment when Congress is not in session. This appointment then expires at the end of the following session. Upon ascending to the White House, George W. Bush renominated Gregory, as well as Terrence Boyle, Helms's hand-picked candidate. The Senate confirmed Gregory but failed to act on Boyle. Bush has now renominated him.

Usually, though, a compromise is arranged, just as there must be if both senators are from the president's party. Nominees must be satisfactory to both senators, though perhaps not the first choice of either, or the two must work out an agreement between them. Even when both senators are from the opposition party, the president may have to come to terms with them. Frequently one side will exchange support for a nomination for backing on a matter the other considers important.

If the president is unable to reach such agreement (or actually for any reason whatsoever), opponents of a nominee can still block an appointment to the lower courts by preventing a floor vote. This maneuver is yet another source of senatorial power in the judicial appointments game. The explicit constitutional requirement of a two-thirds majority for Senate ratification of treaties clearly implies that only a simple majority is required in other circumstances where consent is needed, including the approval of judges. Nevertheless, a minority can keep the Senate from "consenting" to judicial appointment through extended debate, known as a filibuster. Short of unanimous consent, such debate can be ended only by invoking cloture, a formal motion to close debate. Under current Senate rules, cloture requires the concurrence of sixty senators, leaving a mere forty-one senators the power to thwart a vote if they so choose.

As far as we can tell, prior to 1968 the Senate never invoked the filibuster to block a judicial nominee. In that year, a coalition of Republicans and conservative southern Democrats, hopeful that Richard Nixon would take the presidency in the fall election, prevented a vote over Abe Fortas, an associate justice whom Lyndon Johnson was attempting to promote to the position of chief justice. Three decades later, during the Clinton administration, Republicans blocked numerous nominees from coming for a vote before the Senate, but usually through the failure of the Judiciary Committee to approve, or even consider, the candidate—not via a filibuster. So while the Judiciary Committee granted hearings to over 90 percent of the president's circuit court nominees when it was under Democratic control during Clinton's first two years in office, that figure dropped to 74 percent, 79 percent, and finally to 47 percent in the Republican-led Senates of 1995–1996, 1997–1998, and 1999–2000, respectively.

That these Clinton nominees failed to obtain hearings, which are a near requisite for a floor vote to occur, under Republican control of the Senate demonstrates the power of a majority party at work. During the first term of the George W. Bush administration, though, it was the minority party, the Democrats, that blocked ten lower court nominations via filibusters (Bush renominated seven during his second term).

Many reasons exist for this largely unprecedented use of judicial filibusters, but surely among them is the fact that filibusters no longer bring the work of the Senate to a halt. Fans of *Mr. Smith Goes to Washington* may recall that the whole Senate shut down while Mr. Smith led his filibuster. No more. Senate practice since the 1970s permit Senate business to take place along multiple tracks, allowing other work to go on. And those wishing to filibuster no longer need to hold the floor. Thus, by making the filibuster less destructive to the Senate and less onerous to those carrying it out, Senate rules also make filibusters more likely.[18]

In response, and with their eyes on at least one Supreme Court vacancy, Republicans now claim that filibustering judicial nominations violates the constitutional requirement of "advice and consent." Of course, that some of these same Republicans voted against cloture for Clinton nominees is no more surprising than the fact that Democrats now supporting the filibuster insisted on the right to a floor vote when Clinton was president. "The Senate is surely under no obligation to confirm any particular nominee . . . but it should vote him up or vote him down," said Patrick Leahy (D-Vt.) during the Clinton years.[19] At the time, of course, many of his fellow Democrats concurred, but now those same words come out of the mouths of Senate Republicans, not to mention President Bush himself.

While motions to change the filibuster rules are themselves subject to filibuster, a *constitutional* challenge to the Senate's rules can be decided by a simple majority of that body. This so-called nuclear option would

change Senate rules by allowing a simple majority to bring judicial nominations to the floor for a vote, without the sixty-vote supermajority currently needed to end debate. In the spring of 2005 a compromise reached
by moderate Democrats and Republicans, which allowed three of seven
filibustered judicial nominees to come to the floor for a vote, forestalled a
threatened vote on the nuclear option—at least for now, and so long as
Democrats limit judicial filibusters to "extraordinary circumstances."

The Role of Politics, Partisanship, and Ideology

In short, whatever the arguments about the framers' intent, it is clear that
the arrangement they devised, presidential nomination followed by Senate confirmation, as well as the parts of the process they did not, such as
senatorial courtesy, have worked to give senators a crucial role in the process of judicial appointments. If history is any indication, it is quite un-
likely that they will demote themselves anytime soon.

Practice and time also have settled the issue of the role of politics in
judicial appointments. However loud the critics may be, the simple reality
is that both the Senate and the president take into account nominees' partisanship and ideology, in addition to their professional qualifications, when
they make their decisions, and they always have. The evidence is too overwhelming to ignore.

Since we spend much of this book considering that evidence, suffice it to
supply here only a small piece: the role of partisanship in judicial appointments. Since the expansion of the federal judiciary in the mid-nineteenth
century, presidents have looked to their own party to make appointments
to the federal bench. Grover Cleveland, Woodrow Wilson, and Ronald
Reagan virtually never nominated a person outside of their own political
party; even the Democrat Jimmy Carter, who was more willing than any
other president in this period to look beyond partisan boundaries, made
only 16 percent of his appointments to Republicans. Indeed, across the
entire 135-year period, 92.5 percent of all 3,082 appointments to the lower
federal courts (through 2004) have gone to candidates affiliating with the
president's party.

The picture for the Supreme Court is no different. When George Washington proceeded to offer all fourteen of his nominations to Federalists, he
initiated a trend that continues today. All but seventeen of the 147 candidates for a position on the nation's highest court belonged to the same

party as the president at the time of nomination. Perhaps even more telling, not since 1971, when Richard Nixon nominated the Virginian Lewis Powell as part of his "southern strategy," has a president made a cross-party appointment.[20]

Of course, affiliating with the same party as the president, or sharing his politics, is hardly a constitutional requirement. In fact, the Constitution lists no qualifications for judicial service. Given the importance of partisanship for an appointment to the federal bench, however, might it not be a de facto requirement? At the very least, sharing the president's party affiliation cannot hurt the cause of those seeking to become a judge or justice. Whether this outcome was intended or even anticipated by the framers is hardly more interesting these days than the fact that it is a fundamental part of the process.

2

Vacancies

Official portrait of Justice Arthur J. Goldberg.
*Lucien LeBreton, Collection of the Supreme
Court of the United States*

When President Lyndon Johnson wanted to appoint his good friend and advisor Abe Fortas to the U.S. Supreme Court in 1965, he faced two problems of no small proportions: Fortas did not want to serve, and no vacancy existed on the High Court. Refusing to allow these seemingly insurmountable obstacles to stand in his way, Johnson used all his powers of persuasion to convince Fortas to accept the nomination and to coax a sitting justice, Arthur Goldberg, to leave the bench. In the case of Fortas, the president simply informed the justice-to-be that he was planning to announce his appointment, and Fortas could accompany him or not. Fortas went along, and within a matter of weeks he took his seat on the Supreme Court. As for Goldberg, Johnson deployed something of a carrot-and-stick strategy, promising to name him the next U.S. ambassador to the United Nations if he quit but allegedly threatening to publicize the justice's improper fund-raising arrangements if he did not. Whether for these reasons or even perhaps because Goldberg thought his new position at the UN would enable him to persuade Johnson to get out of the Vietnam War, the justice took the carrot and in short order became Ambassador Goldberg. Owing in no small part to disagreements with the president over the war, his stint at the UN proved frustrating, and Goldberg left after just three years to return to private practice in New York. The former justice reentered public life only briefly after that, first in 1970 to run for governor of New York—a race he lost handily to the Republican incumbent, Nelson Rockefeller—and again in 1977, when Jimmy Carter asked him to represent the United States at a human rights conference.[1]

From this story emerge several lessons, not the least of which is that the process of appointing judges begins not with the president but with a vacancy on an existing court or, in some instances, a new seat. Without a spot to fill, as Johnson was all too aware, the president cannot make a nomination. And without a nominee, the Senate has no candidate to confirm or reject.

But this story also raises important questions—mainly about the role of politics in generating those vacancies. Arthur Goldberg, who had become a justice in 1962, was only fifty-seven when he resigned his position; he went on to live another twenty-four years. Without pressure from the president, would Goldberg have departed from the Court just three years after joining it? To state the question more broadly, if it is not always or even often a matter of age or health that leads a judge to retire, what does? For some, we can imagine that economic considerations, such as the desire to retire comfortably, play a role. But for Goldberg the answer may lie in politics, in the form of ideology or even partisanship. After all, would the liberal Democrat Goldberg—the party's nominee for governor and before that secretary of labor under the Kennedy administration—even have entertained Johnson's offer if it had come from a conservative Republican? For that matter, would a conservative Republican president even have bothered to tender it?

We can raise the same questions about judicial vacancies that arise not from departures but from new seats. When Congress expands the federal bench, it often points to burgeoning caseloads or populations in particular regions of the country. But there is an argument to be made that these decisions too are often replete with politics. So, for example, is it a matter of happenstance that the largest contemporary expansions of the lower federal courts have coincided with periods of unified government (i.e., when the same political party controls Congress and the presidency)? In 1978, for example, the Democratic Congress authorized the creation of 35 appellate and 117 district court judgeships for the Democratic president,

Jimmy Carter, to fill. Would a Republican Congress have handed Carter such a bonanza—control of the judiciary for the foreseeable future? Henry Hyde (R.-Ill.) thought not. On the floor of the House he said, "I have no objection to the creation of new judgeships. . . . But let us stop fooling the American people. For seven years, while Republican Presidents were in the White House, the Democratic Congress steadfastly refused to create new judgeships. Now that there is a Democrat in the White House, the Congress is rushing to create 145 new judgeships for him to select."[2] We suspect that Hyde is right. Then again, in light of the seemingly plausible explanation Congress offered for this expansion—to reduce the workload of overburdened federal judges, which is the same sort of reason Congress almost always supplies when it creates new seats—the extent to which politics infiltrates these decisions is a matter worthy of consideration.

Departures from the Bench

Not all departures of federal judges and justices come with an incentive such as a UN ambassadorship, of course. Early on in the nation's history, for example, politicians attempted to deploy an impeachment strategy to accomplish much the same ends. Confronted with a judiciary packed with Federalist judges appointed by George Washington and John Adams, Thomas Jefferson and some of his fellow Republicans began a campaign to impeach them. In February 1803 Jefferson asked Congress to remove the Federalist judge John Pickering; he even went so far as to supply legislators with incriminating evidence against the judge. Pickering was an easy mark (he was aged, mentally incompetent, and an alcoholic), but the president's next targets, Samuel Chase and Chief Justice John Marshall, Federalist members of the Supreme Court, would prove far more difficult.

In fact, for reasons that are still a matter of some debate, the president's impeachment strategy failed in both the short and long terms. While the Congress of Jefferson's day did manage to oust one federal judge, the drunkard Pickering, it never pursued Marshall. As for Chase, the House did impeach him, but the Senate dismissed the charges.[3] This refusal to oust a sitting justice was quite consequential. Not only did the Senate foil Jefferson's plans, it also, if implicitly, declined to establish a norm of impeachment, or any other rule that would require judges or justices of one party to resign from their jobs when a different party came to power.

This is not to say that Congress has never resorted to the constitutional mechanism of impeachment to purge the bench of a jurist. The House has voted to impeach, by the required majority vote, thirteen judges, with the Senate voting to convict (by the required two-thirds vote) seven, thereby removing them.[4] Moreover, while Congress has yet to impeach and convict a Supreme Court justice, it came close in the case of Chase (served 1796–1811), and threatened as much against several others, most notably Abe Fortas (1965–1969) and William O. Douglas (1939–1975).

We ought not underestimate the importance of these threats to impeach. They may well work to prevent federal jurists from veering too far from the agenda of the elected government even if that is not an agenda the jurists favor. In the case of Fortas, talk of impeachment, or more likely criminal prosecution for financial irregularities, may have been the chief reason the justice resigned from the bench. But it was probably Fortas's liberal decisions, not his finances, that raised the specter of impeachment. And surely it was politics that motivated congressional attacks on William O. Douglas, whether because of his left-of-center approach to judging or the Republicans' fury over the Senate's refusal to confirm two Nixon nominees to the Supreme Court. We might say the same of any number of investigations conducted by the legislature or the Justice Department. In one way or another, these inquiries may work to hasten the "voluntary" departure of politically problematic judges. Fortas may fall into this category, as do a number of lower court judges whose decisions angered the administration.

On the other hand, we should acknowledge that ideology and partisanship have not figured prominently in most judicial *removals* in the United States. More likely, contemporary victims of impeachment have committed serious ethical or legal transgressions. Paul N. McCloskey (R-Calif.) made this very point in a speech responding to then-Representative Gerald Ford's call for the impeachment of Douglas. "The bulk [of impeachments concern] . . . judicial misconduct, with scattered instances of non-judicial behavior," Representative McCloskey said. "In all cases . . . the non-judicial behavior involved clear violations of criminal or civil law, and not just a 'pattern of behavior' that others might find less than good."[5]

The historical dearth of politically motivated removals may well reflect a norm against them (see Figure 2.1). Or perhaps the need for removal on political grounds is preempted by the use of other methods to rid the bench of irksome jurists or by foresighted behavior on the part of "opposition"

Figure 2.1
When Politics Can Be Deadly:
Departures from the Bench in Some Other Countries

To say that political considerations may drive departures from the bench is not to equate American practice with norms in other societies. In Argentina, incoming leaders regularly impeach or otherwise force judges appointed by their predecessors to leave the bench. Indeed, despite a constitutional guarantee of life tenure, supreme court justices in Argentina keep their jobs for fewer than six years on average. In the United States, justices tend to stay on almost three times longer.

In other societies, methods of ridding the bench of "unfriendly" judges may be even more extreme, up to and including murder. At one point in Colombia's history, at least 20 percent of its judges were threatened with death and 350 judicial officials assassinated—some by drug cartels but others by law enforcement agents and members of the nation's military.

Source: Gretchen Helmke, "The Logic of Strategic Defection: Court-Executive Relations in Argentina Under Dictatorship and Democracy," 96 *American Political Science Review* 292 (2002).

judges. This is a question commentators will continue to debate. What matters for our purposes is that impeachment or even allegations of misbehavior account for but a minute fraction of empty seats on the federal bench—no more than 1 percent, by many accounts. Rather, it is death, elevation to a higher court, retirement, or resignation that generates vacancies in the U.S. judiciary.

Death and, perhaps to a lesser extent, elevation are involuntary reasons for judges to vacate their seats. Why some judges retire or resign, that is, voluntarily choose to relinquish their tenured position, poses a more interesting question. While it is true that presidents can "pull a Johnson" and cut deals with sitting judges, and Congress can help by threatening impeachment or even manufacturing new seats (a subject we cover in the next section), purely voluntary departures are, apart from death, a chief source of vacancies for contemporary presidents and senates. Between 1945 and 2000, 1,271 federal judges willingly gave up their seats. Over that same period Congress created only 572 new judgeships.[6]

So why do federal judges leave? In some sense, the answer is no different for judges than it is for anyone else contemplating retirement: age, health, family concerns, workload, and economics—in other words, personal reasons. Each plays a role in the choice to depart from the bench, though if existing scholarly studies are to be believed, none more so than economic well-being. We do not disagree, but we suspect that political motivations may be a factor as well. At the very least, the Goldberg-Johnson account suggests that we ought not to neglect them.

Economic Motivations

That economics may figure prominently into departure decisions is hardly implausible. Many federal judges, most notably Chief Justice Rehnquist, have long asserted that judicial salaries are so low that they compel jurists to leave the bench for better-paying jobs. "Inadequate compensation seriously compromises the judicial independence fostered by life tenure," Rehnquist has said. "The prospect that low salaries might force judges to return to the private sector rather than stay on the bench risks affecting judicial performance—instead of serving for life, those judges would serve the terms their finances would allow, and they would worry about what awaits them when they return to the private sector."[7]

And yet studies of contemporary departure patterns unearth no significant link between salaries and departures. What they demonstrate instead is a real connection between retirement benefits and departures.

Unlike judicial salaries, which the Constitution prohibits legislators from decreasing, retirement benefits are subject to adjustment—and adjust Congress has done. Prior to 1869, the legislature made no allowance for pensions. When judges and justices died or resigned, they ceased receiving any salary from the federal government. Not surprisingly, horror stories abound of nineteenth-century judges remaining in their jobs well after their mental capacities and health had long diminished. Indeed, one legislator estimated that about a third of the judiciary was "sleeping upon the bench or dying with age." Surely among the one-third was Justice Robert Grier (1846–1870), who, at seventy-five years of age in 1869, was just barely hanging on. By Grier's own admission, he could no longer walk or even hold a pencil; by his colleagues' account, the justice's mind was "getting a little muddy."

While members of Congress could hardly fail to make a connection between the growing "decrepitude" of the bench and the lack of pensions, they initially attempted to address the problem with the politically charged solution of eviscerating the constitutional guarantee of life tenure. Their repeated efforts to do so failed, but in 1869 they did offer some relief: judges who had reached the age of seventy and had served on the bench for at least ten years would receive their existing salary for life upon retirement.

Why Congress chose 1869 as the year to establish pensions is an interesting question. Certainly some commentators suggest that it was out of concern for the legitimacy of the federal bench—especially the Supreme Court. For how long, they asked, would Americans respect a judiciary replete with mentally and physically impaired members? But the balance of the legal community, us included, suspects a far different motive. Introduced into the Senate just four days after the Republican president Grant took office, the original 1869 bill merely increased the size of the Supreme Court from seven to nine. Undoubtedly this was an effort on the part of the Republican Senate to give Grant a gift in the form of appointments to the Court. Republicans in the House thought the gift too small. The version they proposed called not only for an expansion of the Supreme Court but also for the retirement plan that eventually passed. In addition, it included a proviso that invited the president to appoint a successor for any federal judge who reached the age of seventy and did not make clear his intent to retire within a year.

To be sure, House Republicans invoked the rhetoric of legitimacy to justify their plan. "At least two of the present justices of the Supreme Court," they declared, referring to Nelson and Grier, "although they may live for years, will not long be able, by reasons of the infirmities of age, to take their places upon the Supreme bench." Republicans also expressed "concern" for the aging justices:

> It is well known that one of the most [e]minent members of that bench [Grier] is not able today to reach the bench without being borne to it by the hands of others. It is but fit and proper that such a man should be given the opportunity to retire upon his salary, carrying with him his honors of office.

But the minority party refused to take the bait. To House Democrats, the plan was a barely veiled political ploy to accelerate the retirement of unsympathetic judges and replace them with "younger men . . . more fully identified in sympathy and feelings with the current events in the country."

The Democrats were foresighted enough. Once the Republican bill (minus the forced retirement provision) became law, the nation's judges became only too willing to take advantage of its generous provisions. Among the first to relinquish his seat, perhaps not so surprisingly, was the infirm Justice Grier. No less than a week after the new law went into effect, his colleagues urged him to tender his resignation. If he did not, they impressed on him, Congress might rescind the law, since Grier himself was implicated during the debates. Grier took their advice, transmitting a letter of retirement to President Grant on December 15, 1869.[8]

Grier was hardly alone. Between 1869 and 1953 (before the next pension law went into effect) the turnover rate for federal judges and justices was the highest in the precise year in which they qualified for benefits. Prior to the first year of eligibility, the percentage of jurists voluntarily leaving the bench never surpassed 5.6; in that year it was 18.4.

The 1869 law remained in effect until Congress sweetened the pot in 1954 and once again in 1984, making judges eligible to retire at younger ages if they have accumulated more years of service. These latest schemes seem no different in effect, and perhaps in motivation, from the 1869 act. In both instances, judges continued to depart the bench upon qualifying for a pension. Between 1954 and 1983 (that is, before the passage of the 1984 pension law), 32.6 percent of the nation's judges retired just as soon as they met the plan's eligibility requirements. Prior to the year they were eligible for retirement, the turnover rate was never higher than 2.6 percent.

As for the 1984 plan, if the Republican Congress and president (Reagan) who enacted it intended to hasten the departure of scores of federal judges (and judges appointed by a long string of Democrats at that), just as did the Republicans of 1869, they succeeded. The 1984 law has generated the highest turnover rates of all, with over 45 percent of federal judges now leaving the bench as soon as they become eligible for a pension.[9]

Political Motivations

Sherman Minton was one of a rather large number of judges taking nearly instantaneous advantage of twentieth-century pension laws. About a year after Congress passed the 1954 act, the sixty-five-year-old Supreme Court justice acknowledged that he was "slipping fast." As he wrote to Harry Truman, who had appointed him to the bench, "I have to carry a cane now all the time. . . . I find my work very difficult and I don't have the zest for the work that I used to have. So I am firmly convinced that I should retire."[10] This is precisely what Minton did ten months later, when he had accumulated the fifteen years of judicial service necessary to meet the new law's requirement.

Interestingly enough, though, Minton and Justice Grier before him are rather exceptional cases. Pensions are far more likely to motivate lower court judges to retire than Supreme Court justices—a fact masked by data drawn from the entire judiciary, since the number of judges dwarfs the number of justices. While the overall turnover rate (from 1869 to 2002) for district court judges jumps to 39 percent in the year they qualify for retirement benefits, that figure is only 13 percent for Supreme Court justices.

For many justices, then, economic considerations do not tell the whole story. Nor, for that matter, can we say they fully account for the departure of even lower court judges: 39 percent is not 100 percent.

What is missing from this personal, economic account of judicial departures, we believe, is a consideration absent for most working Americans but not for federal judges: politics—or, more pointedly, the idea that judges and justices strategically time their departures to coincide with presidents (and perhaps Senates) who share their partisanship or ideology.

Evidence supporting this view for the nation's trial courts, we readily admit, is mixed. Professor Albert Yoon argues that it is pensions and not politics that motivate district court judges to retire. These judges, he finds, are no more likely to vacate their seat when their party is in power than when it is not. On the other hand, if in fact lawmakers affiliating with, say, the Republican party enact pension laws precisely to encourage the retirement of Democratic judges—think 1869 or perhaps 1984—then Yoon's finding becomes more explicable.

When it comes to the courts of appeals, an extensive search for strategically timed retirements or resignations is hardly necessary, as political scientists have long demonstrated their existence. David Nixon and J. David Haskin tell us that these judges will remain on the bench, even if they are ill or eligible for retirement, to prevent a president from appointing a successor of a different political party. Conversely, they show that when the president and judge share a partisan attachment, the probability of retirement doubles. James F. Spriggs and Paul Wahlbeck, two other political scientists, concur. Their analysis of voluntary departures from the circuits between 1893 and 1991 expects about 1.5 judges to retire each year when they and the president share the same party affiliation, but just 0.5 when they are of different parties. Since only 1.3 retirements occurred per year during this period, the effect of partisanship is sizable indeed.[11]

As for the Supreme Court, even less doubt exists about the role of politics in motivating justices to depart from the bench. Justice Robert Grier may have retired directly after passage of the 1869 pension law, but some of his contemporaries, equally as ill, hung on. Justice Nathan Clifford (1858–1881), who had been eligible for retirement benefits since 1873, refused to retire during a Republican administration despite his seriously declining mental capability. Chief Justice Earl Warren (1953–1969), to take another example, also attempted to time his retirement, in his case so that Lyndon Johnson would be able to name his successor. The liberal Warren retired only conditionally, "at such time as a successor is qualified," in effect threatening to stay on the Court if the Senate refused to confirm his replacement. The Republicans, along with conservative southern Democrats, called Warren's bluff and rejected, through a filibuster, Abe Fortas's promotion to chief justice. Richard Nixon, Warren's longtime nemesis, was then elected president and Warren chose to retire, his scheme to guarantee a liberal successor a failure.

And it has been reported that after CBS News declared Vice President Al Gore the winner in Florida in 2000, the Republican justice Sandra Day O'Connor deemed his victory "terrible." As O'Connor's husband later explained, his wife was planning on retiring but would not want to depart during a Gore presidency. Following the publication of this story and the Court's role in declaring George W. Bush president, O'Connor stayed on the job into the first year of Bush's second term.[12]

Would she have remained on the bench had the Democrats mounted a serious threat to take control of the presidency and Senate in 2004? Chief Justice Rehnquist supplies one answer when he observes that departure decisions based on the nominating president's ideology may not be "one hundred percent true but [are] certainly true in more cases than not, I would think."[13]

O'Connor's seems to be among the "more cases," and Rehnquist's observation is correct more generally. Warren was hardly the last to engage in strategic retirement planning. Nearly every single justice who has left the Court over the least three decades seems to have contemplated the politics surrounding his or her departure (see Figure 2.2). In some instances,

Figure 2.2
Retirements on the Supreme Court since 1975

Justice (Dates of Service)/Circumstances Surrounding Departure

William O. Douglas (1939–1975)

Douglas, in the face of extremely poor health, originally would not retire while Ford, who tried to impeach him, was president. He said Ford would "appoint some bastard." But after a debilitating stroke Douglas succumbed to the inevitable and retired.

Potter Stewart (1958–1981)

According to the Republican Stewart, while he became eligible for retirement in 1980, he did not want the vacancy created by his retirement to become an election issue. So he delayed his retirement until 1981, which, perhaps not so coincidentally, was the year Ronald Reagan replaced Jimmy Carter.

Warren E. Burger (1969–1986)

The *Wall Street Journal* reported that the conservative Republican Burger was "concerned about the coming Senate elections and the possibility that Republicans could lose their majority. A Democratic-controlled Senate would be far less amenable to confirming conservative Reagan-appointed justices." Indeed, the Republican Senate in 1986 overwhelmingly confirmed Rehnquist to replace Burger and unanimously confirmed Scalia to replace Rehnquist. But just one year later a Democratic Senate rejected Robert Bork.

Lewis F. Powell Jr. (1971–1987)

In 1987, Powell's friend and former law clerk John C. Jeffries wrote the conservative Powell a memo explaining why he should vacate his seat while Reagan was president rather than waiting until illness might force him to leave during a Democratic administration. Several days later Powell told Rehnquist of his plans to retire.

William J. Brennan Jr. (1956–1990)

A stroke forced the liberal Brennan to leave the bench. Otherwise he "had no intention" of retiring during George H. W. Bush's presidency.

Thurgood Marshall (1967–1991)

Growing increasingly ill, the liberal Marshall reportedly told his clerks that should he die during the Reagan years, they should "prop him up" and keep on voting. Too sick to wait for the elec-

(continues)

Figure 2.2 (*continued*)

tion of a Democratic president, however, Marshall retired while
George H. W. Bush was in office.

Byron White (1962–1993)

Just six months after Clinton's inauguration, the Democrat White
retired. He had long said he wanted to leave the bench when a
Democrat occupied the White House.

Harry A. Blackmun (1970–1994)

Though appointed by Nixon, Blackmun moved increasingly to the
left during his years on the Court. Wanting to ensure that his replacement would also be a liberal, he waited until a Democrat
won the presidency.

Sandra Day O'Connor (1981–2005)

The press reported that O'Connor was disappointed when she
thought Al Gore won the presidential election of 2000. She remained on the Court to see George W. Bush win a second term,
and has now retired with Republicans in control of the Senate as
well.

William H. Rehnquist (1971–2005?)

At one point Rehnquist was said to have wanted to retire at age
seventy, which would have been in 1994, while Clinton was
president. Now, in 2005, Rehnquist is ill, and Republicans control
the White House and the Senate.

Sources: James E. DiTullio and John B. Schochet, "Saving This Honorable Court: A
Proposal to Replace Life Tenure on the Supreme Court with Staggered, Nonrenewable
Eighteen-Year Terms," 90 *Virginia Law Review* 1093 (2004), and sources cited therein.
See also Artemus Ward, *Deciding to Leave: The Politics of Retirement from the United
States Supreme Court* (2003).

illness foiled their plans—the liberals William O. Douglas, William J.
Brennan Jr. (1956–1990), and Thurgood Marshall (1967–1991) all left the
bench in poor health during Republican administrations. But Lewis Powell
Jr. (1971–1987), Byron White (1962–1993), and Harry A. Blackmun
(1970–1994) succeeded in seeing presidents who were in sync with their
partisan or ideological interests name their successor. Even the conservative Chief Justice Warren E. Burger (1969–1986) achieved what his liberal
predecessor, Earl Warren, could not: the confirmation of an ideologically
compatible heir in William H. Rehnquist.

The Creation of New Seats

At the turn of the nineteenth century, the Federalist-led Congress proposed to restructure the judicial system by establishing new courts (and judges). Federalist legislators told constituents that their proposal to increase the number of courts was necessary "to render the administration of justice more effectual and less burdensome." Likewise, ninety years later, elected officials justified the so-called Evarts Act of 1891, which created circuit courts and authorized some ninety new judgeships, by pointing to the U.S. Supreme Court's overflowing docket. "Something [had] to be done" to relieve the justices, one said.[14]

In neither of these cases were legislators lying to the public when they justified the laws as not merely salutary but necessary. No one then or now argues in favor of an ineffectual, inefficient system of justice. And no one, by the 1890s, could deny that the Supreme Court's caseload had reached new heights. In 1891 the justices decided 252 cases with a written opinion, nearly 180 more cases than just thirty years earlier. On the other hand, it seems entirely implausible that the precise timing of these bench expansions was not motivated by the sheer desire of one political party to pack the courts. The Federalists running the legislature passed their bill, the Judiciary Act of 1801, on February 13—just four days before they would cede control of Congress and watch the inauguration of the Republican Thomas Jefferson. Seeing the 1801 Act for the political ploy that it surely was, the Republicans quickly repealed it.[15] As for the 1891 Evarts Act, while not necessarily unwise, it was quite the political triumph. Republicans, who controlled both Houses and the presidency, enacted the bill on March 3, 1891—just a day before Democrats would take over the House (but not the Senate or the White House). Accordingly, Republicans were able to expand the bench while their party was in power and then, because they controlled the presidency and the Senate, fill the new seats with partisans. Had Republicans waited even another day, the new Democratic majority in the House might have blocked their effort.

That politics played a role in generating these laws, at least a role far greater than the legislators let on, is as understandable as it is predictable. After all, while departures from the bench may be the primary source of vacancies, waiting for a sitting judge to die or retire is hardly the most efficient way for political actors to gain control of the U.S. judiciary.

Expanding the bench by authorizing the creation of new seats, as legislators did in 1801 and 1891, on the other hand, is a paradigm of political expediency. This is especially so if the political party in control of government is different from the party in control of the bench. Under those circumstances—actually, precisely the circumstances that would make control of the courts desirable and plausible—judges who belong to the opposition party may be especially reluctant to retire.

Such was the position in which Democrat Franklin D. Roosevelt found himself in 1937. Roosevelt was eager to pass new laws designed to improve economic conditions and ameliorate the plight of individuals affected by the Great Depression of 1929. Confronted with a Supreme Court that consistently struck down this New Deal legislation—and with justices who showed no interest in retiring—FDR asked the Democratic Congress to pass the now infamous court-packing plan. The president's idea was to expand the number of lower court judgeships and adopt a flexible method of temporarily moving lower court judges from their normal duties to districts with case backlogs. But these administrative reforms were little more than a smoke screen for FDR's Supreme Court proposals. He wanted Congress to authorize the creation of one new seat on the Supreme Court for every justice who had attained the age of seventy but remained in active service. These expanded positions would have an upper limit of six, bringing the potential size of the Court to a maximum of fifteen. At the time of his proposal, six sitting justices were older than seventy.

In Roosevelt's case, his party was already in firm control of the presidency and legislature. His intent was to bring the "obstructionist" third branch into the fold. The political circumstances surrounding the enactment of the 1801 and 1891 acts were somewhat different—the Federalists of 1801, for example, already had captured the judiciary and only wanted to strengthen their hold before ceding the rest of the government to their opponents. And yet all three episodes share a crucial political feature: in each case, the party proposing the bench expansion would be able to name the new judges.

This is hardly an unusual circumstance. Since the Judiciary Act of 1789, in which Congress established the first federal judicial system, legislators have expanded the appellate bench with fervor. The initial 1789 act authorized the creation of only nineteen U.S. judgeships—six for the Supreme Court and thirteen for the district courts. (No separate appellate court judges were necessary since the three circuit courts established by the new Congress were staffed by a district judge and two justices of the Supreme Court.) By 2005 Congress had authorized the creation of more than 800 judgeships: 3 new seats on the Supreme Court, 179 on the courts of appeals, and 652 on the district courts.[16]

To be sure, Congress authorized these expansions at very different moments in American history—during economic busts and booms, in times of war and peace, and when Democrats and Republicans occupied the White House. But, like the expansion plans of 1801, 1891, and 1937, most came about when one party held the presidency and majorities in the legislature. The number of authorized positions on the U.S. Supreme Court, after initially being set at six, has grown three times, in 1807 (to seven), 1837 (to nine), and 1863 (to ten). In all three instances the same political party controlled Congress and the presidency, and in all three instances politics was a driving force behind the adjustment. The creation of a tenth justice in 1863, for example, reflected Congress's desire to provide President Abraham Lincoln with an opportunity to appoint a justice who would favor the Union's interests.

Now, of course, the size of the Court is nine, not ten. But even behind that contraction lies a story of political intrigue. To prevent the Democrat Andrew Johnson from making an appointment to the Court, the Radical Republican Congress of 1866 passed legislation requiring the number of justices to diminish to seven before a president could make an appointment. Just ten days after Johnson's term had expired and the Republican Ulysses Grant was inaugurated, Congress passed the Judiciary Act of 1869. In addition to establishing pensions for judges, the law increased the size of the Court to nine, thereby enabling Grant to make an appointment.

Similar political patterns repeat themselves over authorizations for expansions of the federal appellate bench. An astonishingly high proportion of the authorizations—thirty-two of the thirty-seven, or 86.5 percent—were enacted during political periods when the same party held a majority in Congress and controlled the White House. To think about it another way, since 1869 one party has led government for ten periods. In nine of those ten periods, Congress has added new seats to the circuits (the exception was during World War I). All in all, a unified government increases the likelihood of an appellate bench expansion by over 50 percent, even after accounting for the judiciary's workload.

This is not to say, we hasten to note, that workload or other efficiency concerns have played no role in Congress's decision to create new seats. But the effect is muted. As the law scholars John M. de Figueiredo and Emerson Tiller demonstrate, it takes an additional 6,500 cases in the circuits (since the last bench expansion) to match the effect of a unified government. Only since the 1980s has an increase of this magnitude occurred.[17]

The lack of a robust association between appellate bench expansion and workload, however, has not deterred politicians from referencing overburdened judges (or growth in the United States) to rationalize increasing the size of the U.S. judiciary. They did as much in 1801 and 1891, and the rhetoric continues today. To justify their plan to split the U.S. Court of Appeals for the Ninth Circuit into two or even three circuits and create new judgeships in the process, Republican members of the current Congress point to the "booming populations" in states served by the Ninth, the "terrible backlog of appeals that have built up" there, and "the impact that the resulting delays are having on case law and the lives of real people."[18]

These sorts of claims are, of course, hard to refute. Since 1789, the United States has grown exponentially, from the eleven states that ratified the Constitution to its current fifty, from a nation of just 891,000 square miles in size in 1790 to 3.79 million now, and from a population of 3.9 million at the time of America's founding to its present 281 million. With the addition of states and territory has come the need to create new courts or to split existing circuits. With the increase in population, among other factors, has come an increase in use of the courts that too has seemed to necessitate new judicial seats to handle the workload. Even calls to divide the Ninth Circuit appear reasonable enough. That circuit covers more states than any other circuit. It also houses more judges and conducts more business than any other. It is has more than double the number of authorized judges than the next largest circuit (twenty-eight for the Ninth versus seventeen for the Fifth). And despite their circuit's size, jurists on the Ninth may work harder than most. On average, they terminate 490 cases on their merits per year, about 60 more than in each of the eleven others. Finally, the Ninth has far more than its fair share of federal litigation, with over 21 percent (14,274 out of 67,762) of the nation's appeals filed there.

However convincing these facts and figures sound, they no more dupe Democrats in 2005 than did the Democrats' arguments about overworked judges fool Henry Hyde and other Republicans in 1978. In both instances, legislators saw the "facts" for what they were: political moves on the part of the opposition party to pack the courts. In the case of the Ninth, Democrats realize that dividing the circuit would permit George W. Bush and the Republican Senate to fill the new judgeships created as part of the split. It also would enable them to break up what is among the most liberal circuits in the country.[19] Democrats have, unsurprisingly, opposed the split.[20] But at the end of the day, the Democrats may not prevail: if history is any indication, arguments about the need for "expediency" and "justice," especially when reinforced with plausible data, can be very persuasive to Americans.

But not always. Franklin Roosevelt predicated his court-packing plan of 1937 at least in part on the argument that the judiciary was too overworked and understaffed to carry out its duties effectively. "By bringing into the Judiciary system a steady and continuing stream of new and younger blood," Roosevelt said, "I hope . . . to make the administration of all Federal justice speedier and, therefore, less costly."[21] But in this case the efficiency argument failed. Despite Roosevelt's popularity and his overwhelming majorities in Congress, just five months after he proposed the plan the Senate Judiciary Committee recommended against passage of the Court-packing bill. To the president's great displeasure, seven of the ten senators signing the report were Democrats. Even a last-ditch compromise effort—a plan that would have raised the threshold age for replacing the justices from seventy to seventy-five years—broke down after its major supporter, majority leader Joseph Robinson (D-Ark.), died from a heart attack.

Why did FDR fail when so many others before (and after him) succeeded? One answer is that public reaction to his plan was not favorable. Polls taken during the course of the debate over the plan revealed that at no time did a majority of Americans approve of Roosevelt's proposal. In fact, as the battle raged on, the public grew even less supportive of what it viewed as a politically motivated effort to tamper with the structure of government.[22]

Another answer is that FDR did not fail: he lost only the battle over the court-packing plan, not the larger war over the judiciary's support for his New Deal legislation. After years of striking down virtually every New Deal plan that came its way, mostly by votes of 5–4, the Court—or, rather, one justice—seemed to have a change of heart. On April 12, 1937, less than two months after Roosevelt had proposed the court-packing scheme, the justices upheld a major piece of New Deal legislation and, in so doing, ushered in a new era in the constitutional relationship between the government and the economy.

This famous "switch in time that saved nine" took the energy out of Roosevelt's drive to add new justices. No longer did it appear necessary, as the Court now was looking with greater approval at federal (and state) legislation to correct the failing economy. In addition, on May 18, 1937, Justice Van Devanter, a consistent foe of Roosevelt's New Deal programs, announced that he would retire from the Court at the end of the term. Finally the president would have an opportunity to put a justice of his own choosing on the Court. He would eventually appoint nine during his twelve years in office—still a record among twentieth-century presidents.[23]

Whether Roosevelt succeeded or failed, what role public opinion played in the debate, and the extent to which Robinson's death affected the outcome of congressional debates are questions scholars continue to debate— even if they seem no closer to resolving them now than fifty years ago. What is clear to most observers, though, is that FDR's proposal, while extraordinary in its hubris, was a product of the very same factors that nearly always leads to vacancy-creation schemes: politics, plain and simple.

3

Nominating Federal Judges and Justices

Official portrait of Justice Abe Fortas. *George Augusta, Collection of the Supreme Court of the United States*

That Lyndon Johnson induced Justice Arthur Goldberg to retire in 1965 may have surprised many. That he named Abe Fortas to replace Goldberg could not have surprised anyone. Back in 1948, when Johnson was running for the Senate, he called upon Fortas's legal acumen to secure "Landslide Lyndon's" eighty-seven-vote victory in the face of clear evidence of voter fraud by the Johnson campaign. The two became and remained close friends. But Fortas was more than that. He was a brilliant attorney, perhaps the "the best lawyer in America."[1] Moreover, Fortas was a New Deal liberal who shared Johnson's views on race, poverty, and governmental actions to remedy them. Fortas was Johnson's most trusted advisor, and the president was fully intent on placing him on the Court.

LBJ was hardly the first president to use the power of appointment to name a friend to the federal bench. George Washington too conferred judicial positions on personal associates, and 150 years later Harry Truman famously nominated four close pals to the Supreme Court: Harold Burton, Fred Vinson, Tom Clark, and Sherman Minton. Overall, about three-fifths of those seated on the Supreme Court personally knew the president who put them there.

Undoubtedly, however, presidents have other objectives—mainly political objectives—in mind when they make judicial nominations. In some instances, they use their appointments to shore up electoral support for their party or themselves—what we might call electoral or partisan goals. When Ronald Reagan nominated Sandra Day O'Connor to the Supreme Court in 1981, he was not appointing a crony; he had met her only once, and that was six days before he nominated her. Rather, Reagan was seeking to fulfill a campaign promise to appoint a woman to the Court—a promise he no doubt felt would further his and his party's chances of attracting female voters.[2] In other instances, policy or ideological goals move to the fore. Abe Fortas may have been a longtime friend of the president, but he also was an ideological soul mate—a liberal who LBJ thought would help advance the administration's policy goals once on the Court.

That virtually all presidents have sought to advance personal or, more likely, political goals when choosing judges and justices does not mean that they are entirely unfettered.[3] While, to be sure, the framers of the Constitution expected the new nation's chief executive to play a crucial role in naming federal judges—they did, after all, list the power of appointment in Article II, that is, among the *president's* powers—those same framers gave the Senate an equally crucial role: the power to consent to the president's choices. Because it is the Senate, not the president, that has the final say on nominees, that body can impose an effective restraint on the president's choices even if it does not completely control the selection of those candidates.

Since presidents desire to see the successful appointment of their nominees, the need for Senate confirmation is hardly a constraint they can afford to ignore—and most have not. In making their selections, presidents have taken into account not only their own personal and political goals but those of senators as well. Because the professional qualifications of the nominee are of nearly threshold importance for the senators whose favorable votes they are trying to court, and perhaps for themselves as well, presidents have generally attempted (though not always successfully) to select people of competence and integrity. A candidate's ideology and partisanship too are crucial to senators. If they and the candidate are ideologically incompatible, then the odds of nay votes skyrocket. As a result, the political leanings of the Senate must also become a part of the president's calculus, perhaps compelling him to nominate a second- or third-choice candidate, or one even further down on his list of possibilities. When presidents ignore the Senate altogether the likelihood of rejection increases, meaning that they might find themselves in the uncomfortable position of having to make two or even three nominations for the same seat. Such was the fate of Johnson's successor, Richard Nixon, who put forth the names of two nominees before he found one, in Harry Blackmun, who would pass muster with the Senate. As for Johnson himself—the "Master of the Senate," as some call him—a compromise was not necessary: the Senate of 1965 confirmed his dear friend Fortas by a voice vote. The 1965 nomination may be one example where the president's choice would have been exactly the same even if the Constitution provided him with unilateral appointment power.

Judges and Presidents

Without a doubt, presidents have strong incentives to concern themselves with appointments to the federal bench. For some, the nomination of particular kinds of judges can work to fulfill campaign promises.[4] In 1860, when running for president, Abraham Lincoln implied that he would appoint judges opposed to slavery. During his bid for the presidency in 1980, Reagan pledged to nominate the first woman justice. In an effort to bring the then-solid Democratic South into the Republican fold, Richard Nixon committed to appointing strict constructionists who would (in contrast to the liberal Warren Court) interpret the law, not make it. Nearly four decades later, during the 2004 presidential debates, George W. Bush repeated the Nixon mantra:

> The voters will know I'll put competent judges on the bench, people who will strictly interpret the Constitution and will not use the bench to write social policy. And that's going to be a big difference between my opponent and me. I believe that . . . the judges ought not to take the place of the legislative branch of government, that they're appointed for life and that they ought to look at the Constitution as sacred. They shouldn't misuse their bench.[5]

Appointment is the only mechanism at a president's disposal that can alter the composition of the federal bench. While the chief executive alone cannot add judges or remove recalcitrant ones, as he may well do with wayward members of the cabinet, he can work to ensure that his nominees share his (and, presumably, the electorate's) political values. It is this link that explains why a number of legal commentators were disturbed by the

Supreme Court's decisive vote in the election of 2000. As the Yale law scholar Bruce Ackerman famously put it:

> In our democracy, there is one basic check on a runaway court: *presidential elections*. And a majority of the justices [in *Bush v. Gore*] conspired to eliminate this check. The Supreme Court cannot be permitted to arrange for its own succession. . . . When sitting justices retire or die, the Senate should refuse to confirm any nomination offered by President Bush. . . . The right-wing bloc on the Court should not be permitted to extend its control for a decade or more simply because it has put George W. Bush into the White House.[6]

While the opportunity for the Senate to reject Ackerman's proposal, as it inevitably will, has only recently arisen, that body has hardly been hesitant to confirm George W. Bush's lower court nominees. In Bush's first four years the president made thirty-six appointments to federal appellate courts, meaning that as of May 2005 slightly more than one out of every five sitting circuit court judges were his nominees.[7] Bush's appointees already constitute a majority (six of eleven judges) on the Eighth Circuit, which covers the states of Arkansas, Iowa, Minnesota, Missouri, Nebraska, North Dakota, and South Dakota.

These figures demonstrate just how quickly a president can change the composition of the bench, and, assuming he selects carefully, the extent to which he can reap the benefits of such appointments during his tenure. In light of the thousands and thousands of cases to which the federal government is a party or is otherwise interested each year, these benefits, mostly in the form of a packed judiciary likely to support his policies, are no small matter to the president.

Without doubt, then, presidents have strong incentives to pay heed to the men and women they appoint to the nation's bench. At the same time, it is true that most administrations have been more attentive to some judicial appointments than others. Even though he was a lawyer, Bill Clinton was, with some notable exceptions here and there, relatively disinterested in appointments to the lower courts. When it came to the two vacancies he filled on the Supreme Court, though, Clinton participated in almost every stage in the process, from attending initial meetings with his staff to generating lists of names and interviewing the candidates he eventually selected, Ruth Bader Ginsburg (1993–) and Stephen Breyer (1994–).[8]

That Clinton was personally involved in the selection of Ginsburg and Breyer is not altogether surprising. Nearly without exception, presidents dedicate more time to appointments to higher courts than to the district courts. Several reasons exist for this, not the least of which is sheer numbers. Over the course of one four-year term, a president may make well over a hundred nominations to the district courts. Devoting careful and sustained attention to each and every one would be virtually impossible in light of his other responsibilities. On the other hand, opportunities to make an appointment to the Supreme Court are fairly rare events in contemporary times. During his eight years in office, Bill Clinton made only two. With Justice O'Connor's retirement, George W. Bush, now into his second term, has only just acquired the opportunity to make one, and he will undoubtedly give careful consideration to the ultimate choice, just as did most of his predecessors.[9]

The relative number of nominations is not the only factor affecting whether the president personally will devote time to selecting judges. The comparative influence of the courts themselves also is crucial. Because the geographic jurisdictions of the lower courts are limited—to a state or just part of it, in the case of the district courts, or to several states, in the case of circuit courts—their rulings hold only for that geographic area. So if, say, a district court strikes down a federal law, that decision is valid in that district only. In contrast, if the Supreme Court, with its national jurisdiction, renders a law unconstitutional, its ruling binds all other courts and the other two branches of government as well. From the president's point of view, then, the limited influence of district courts and to a lesser extent the circuits will lead him to delegate some of his appointment power to advisors. Moreover, since appellate courts can reverse the decisions of district courts, and the Supreme Court can reverse the appellate courts, the higher the court, the more influential it is as a legal policy maker. Thus, the higher the court, the more consequential it is to the president. Then there is the matter of the Senate's role in the process. As we discussed in Chapter 1, the higher the court, the more discretion the president has to make nominations that reflect his preferences. The lower the court, the more influence the Senate expects, at least at the nomination stage.

Do not take this to mean, however, that the president lacks strong preferences about whom he would like to see serve on the nation's lower courts. Quite the opposite. In a perfect, unconstrained world, his appointments at all levels of the judicial hierarchy would reflect precisely his administration's (largely political) goals. In reality, the president may have objectives he would like to accomplish via appointments to the bench, but he is not an unconstrained actor who can make decisions based entirely on his own preferences. Rather, when it comes to making his selections, the president must be strategic. To achieve his goals he must take into account the preferences and likely actions of the body that must confirm his nominees, the Senate, as well as certain norms senators expect him to follow. If he does not, he runs the risk of seeing his candidates defeated, in which case he cannot accomplish his objectives, whatever they might be. Both parts of this claim—the president's goals and the constraints he confronts in attempting to achieve them—deserve some consideration.

Presidential Goals

In anticipation of one or more retirements from the U.S. Supreme Court, the Bush administration compiled a list of potential replacements. The possible candidates are mostly sitting judges but do include a few politicians and members of the executive branch (see Figure 3.1).

If Bush's predecessors are any indication, a range of actors contributed to his list. Certainly some, perhaps the vast majority, came from inside the executive branch—perhaps even from the president himself. As previously noted, Bill Clinton was actively engaged in the process of generating candidates for the appointments that eventually went to Ginsburg and Breyer, as were Lyndon Johnson and Richard Nixon before him. We have no reason to suspect that Bush is any different; at the very least, he is surely familiar with many of the oft-mentioned candidates, including two that he appointed to positions in the executive branch: former solicitor general Theodore Olson and attorney general (formerly White House counsel) Alberto Gonzales.

Beyond the president and his advisors, trusted senators, party leaders, and organized interests recommended at least some of the names under consideration. Interest groups, in particular, have figured prominently into Bush's appointments to the lower courts. No group has been more involved than the Federalist Society, an organization devoted to counterbalancing what it decries as the "orthodox liberal" ideology that "dominates" the legal community. Of the George W. Bush administration's first seventy

Figure 3.1
Names Mentioned as Possible Bush Nominees
to the U.S. Supreme Court

Name (Age)	Current Position	Partisanship	Comments
Alito, Samuel A. (50)	U.S. Court of Appeals (3rd)	Republican; appointed by G. H. W. Bush	White male; worked in the Reagan Justice Department; nicknamed "Scalito" or "Scalia-lite"
BeVier, Lillian Riemer (mid-60s)	Law professor (U. Virginia)	Declines to give party affiliation but says she is more "conservative than liberal"; contributor to Republican campaigns	White female; nominated to the Board of the Legal Services Corporation by G. W. Bush; serves on national board of the Federalist Society
Brown, Janice (56)	U.S. Court of Appeals (D.C.)	Republican; appointed by G. W. Bush	Would be first black female justice; appellate court nomination blocked for two years by Democrats; worked on California governor Pete Wilson's campaign
Clement, Edith Brown (57)	U.S. Court of Appeals (5th)	Republican; appointed by G. W. Bush	White female; former District Court judge (G. H. W. Bush appointee); was a maritime attorney prior to ascending to the federal bench
Easterbrook, Frank (57)	U.S. Court of Appeals Judge (7th)	Republican; appointed by Reagan	White male; former law professor; a leading disciple of the law and economics movement
Estrada, Miguel (44)	Lawyer	Presumed Republican (contributor to Republican campaigns, including Bush's)	Male; would be first Hispanic justice; clerked for Anthony Kennedy; contributor to Bush campaign; nominated by G. W. Bush to the D.C. circuit but not confirmed
Garza, Emilio M. (58)	U.S. Court of Appeals (5th)	Republican; appointed by G. H. W. Bush	Male; would be first Hispanic justice; Texan
Gonzales, Alberto (50)	U.S. attorney general	Republican; appointed by G. W. Bush	Male; would be first Hispanic justice; served as general counsel to Governor G. W. Bush and White House counsel to President G. W. Bush

(continues)

Figure 3.1 (*continued*)

Name (Age)	Current Position	Partisanship	Comments
Jones, Edith (56)	U.S. Court of Appeals (5th)	Republican; appointed by Ronald Reagan	White female; Texan; considered by G. H. W. Bush for the position that ultimately went to Souter
Kozinski, Alex (55)	U.S. Court of Appeals (9th)	Republican; appointed by Ronald Reagan	White male; clerked for chief justice Warren Burger and Justice Kennedy (as a circuit court judge)
Kyl, Jon (63)	U.S. senator (Arizona)	Republican	White male; chair of the Senate Republican Policy Committee; member of the Senate Judiciary Committee
Luttig, J. Michael (51)	U.S. Court of Appeals (4th)	Republican; appointed by G. H. W. Bush	White male; clerked for Antonin Scalia; helped shepherd Clarence Thomas through his confirmation proceedings
McConnell, Michael (50)	U.S. Court of Appeals (10th)	Republican; appointed by G. W. Bush	White male; clerked for William Brennan; former law professor; contributor to Bush campaign
Niemeyer, Paul (64)	U.S. Court of Appeals (4th)	Republican; appointed by G. H. W. Bush	White male; Reagan appointee to a U.S. district court before Bush elevated him
Olson, Theodore (55)	Lawyer	Republican	White male; represented Bush in *Bush v. Gore* (2000); G. W. Bush's former U.S. solicitor general
Randolph, A. Raymond (62)	U.S. Court of Appeals (D.C.)	Republican; appointed by G. H. W. Bush	White male; served in Justice Department during the Nixon and Ford administrations
Roberts, John G. (50)	U.S. Court of Appeals (D.C.)	Republican; appointed by G. W. Bush	White male; clerked for William Rehnquist; associate counsel to Reagan
Scalia, Antonin (69)	Supreme Court Justice	Republican; appointed by Ronald Reagan	White male; allegedly campaigning for the chief justice position through public talks and lectures
Smith, Jerry E. (59)	U.S. Court of Appeals (5th)	Republican; appointed by Ronald Reagan	White male; served as city attorney for Houston, Texas
Thomas, Clarence (57)	Supreme Court Justice	Republican; appointed by G. H. W. Bush	Male; would be first black chief justice

Figure 3.1 (*continued*)

Name (Age)	Current Position	Partisanship	Comments
Wilkinson, J. Harvie III (61)	U.S. Court of Appeals (4th)	Republican; appointed by Reagan	White male; clerked for Lewis Powell; former law professor
Williams, Karen (51)	U.S. Court of Appeals (4th)	Republican; appointed by G. H. W. Bush	White female; was in private practice for 12 years prior to her appointment to the Fourth Circuit

Other possible names that have surfaced since Sandra Day O'Connor announced her retirement from the Court include: Danny Boggs, Jose Cabranes, Raoul Cantero III, Ricardo Hinojosa, Edward Prado, and Sonia Sotomayor. All but Cantero are federal judges. Cantero is a justice on the Florida Supreme Court.

nominees, twenty were "recommended directly" by this organization. Even more to the point, several of the candidates have ties to the society, including Michael McConnell, who served as an advisor to the group; a current justice, Antonin Scalia, speaks at some of its functions; and Edith Clement has sat on its advisory council.[10]

Perhaps the Bush administration has even consulted (or been lobbied by) sitting justices or judges, which would certainly not be without precedent. In the 1850s, the entire Supreme Court asked President Franklin Pierce to appoint John Campbell to the bench. Over a century later, as John Dean (of Watergate fame) tells it, Chief Justice Warren Burger "constantly supplied [the administration] with names" for "his" court. When Richard Nixon was attempting to fill two vacancies in 1971, Burger suggested Herschel Friday, an Arkansas attorney who had a connection to Justice Harry Blackmun, a childhood friend of Burger's. At the same time, Burger lobbied against the appointment of a woman—so much so that Nixon's attorney general, John Mitchell, dreaded telling Burger that Mildred Lillie, a California state judge, was on the president's list.[11]

Though Nixon did not appoint Lillie, neither did he nominate Burger's candidate, Friday. In fact, according to Dean, only the president himself and Mitchell knew that William H. Rehnquist would get the nod. All other advisors were kept out of the loop until the last possible moment.

But why Rehnquist and not Friday, Lillie, or any of the other dozen or more prospective nominees Nixon considered? More generally, why do certain names and not others make initial lists, why will some candidates advance in the process to an even shorter list, and why will one ultimately rise above the pack? We could ask the same questions about nominations to the lower courts as well, for even though the president must pay more heed to names submitted by U.S. senators, he and his advisors typically must still make a selection from among an array of choices. What criteria do they use?

The answer to this question lies at least in part with the administration's goals. Undoubtedly, as we hinted above, judicial appointments can work to accomplish many aims, but almost all fall under the rubric of politics. In some instances, politics has centered largely on partisan aims, with the idea being that the president attempts to exploit judicial appointments to advance his or his party's interests; in other cases, politics has been primarily about policy, or the notion that the president seeks to nominate judges and justices who share his political or ideological preferences. Each merits discussion, though, frankly, they are often difficult to separate.

Partisan and Electoral Goals

In some sense it seems odd to think that judicial appointments could help advance the president's and his party's ambitions, electoral or otherwise. After all, most Americans lack even a passing familiarity with courts and judges; they cannot, for example, identify the office Chief Justice William H. Rehnquist holds, much less name any of the other justices. Even more to the point, when asked before the 2004 presidential election, "What issue or problem . . . is most important for the next president to address?" fewer than 0.5 percent said, "The Supreme Court." Of the lower courts, the North Carolina senator Jesse Helms said it best: "You go out on the street of Raleigh, N.C., and ask 100 people, 'Do you give a damn who is on the Fourth Circuit Court of Appeals?' They'll say, 'What's that?'"[12]

On the other hand, when judges or their decisions attract media attention Americans not only are aware of the controversy but also may have strong opinions that they occasionally express in their ballots. The storm over George H. W. Bush's nomination of Clarence Thomas in 1991 provides a case in point. After initial public opinion polls indicated that blacks overwhelmingly believed Thomas when he said he had not sexually harassed Anita Hill, several senators from states with large minority populations voted to confirm Thomas. But some paid a price. Wyche Fowler

(D-Ga.), for one, was defeated at least in part because pro-choice white women were unhappy with his support for the anti-*Roe* Thomas, and Arlen Specter (R.-Penn.) nearly lost his reelection bid, receiving only 49.1 percent of the two-party vote in 1992, compared with 56.4 percent in his previous election, in 1986.[13] Across the United States, voters who disapproved of Thomas were 14 percent more likely to vote for the challenger than the incumbent. On the other hand, voters who disapproved of Thomas were 18.6 percent more likely to vote for their senator if she or he failed to back Thomas.

Clearly, it is not in the president's or, more precisely, his party's interest to see his senators lose support or even go down in defeat over judicial nominees. Even so, the Thomas appointment is hardly a prototypical example of how partisan considerations can come to the fore in the selection of federal judges. (Actually, that appointment was probably something of an anomaly. Owing primarily to charges of sexual harassment, it was a highly visible confirmation battle for a seat on the nation's most visible tribunal, the U.S. Supreme Court.) More typically, the link between judicial nominations and the president's achievement of partisan goals is less direct and can play out in a multitude of ways. In making his appointments to the lower courts, Franklin D. Roosevelt often contemplated how they might help shore up approval for his policies among Democrats within the Senate. So, for example, knowing that he would need the support of the Senate's Foreign Relations Committee as World War II approached, FDR nominated a candidate suggested by the committee's chair over one proposed by the other senator from the state where the vacancy arose. Roosevelt apparently felt he had to accommodate the chair to ensure approval of his war policies.[14] The Eisenhower and Kennedy administrations used their appointment power somewhat differently. They tried to strengthen their respective parties, with both Ike and JFK occasionally supporting candidates proposed by competitors within their party.

Other presidents have placed a great deal of weight on geography at least in part to advance their or their party's electoral objectives. Richard Nixon was nearly obsessed with making appointments that would help his 1972 reelection bid, and in particular, as we noted earlier, with enhancing the Republican party's appeal to southerners by appointing a justice from that region. And Nixon was surely not the first.

Prior to 1891, geographical concerns were particularly paramount because the justices "rode circuit." The Judiciary Act of 1789 divided the nation into six circuits, then corresponding to the number of seats on the Supreme Court. As the number of circuits increased, so also did the number of justices. Each justice served in a dual capacity: as a circuit court judge and as a member of the Supreme Court. The assumption from the beginning was that the justice would reside within the circuit he served, thereby initiating a tradition of regional representation. As George Washington wrote in 1799, when it appeared that a vacancy would arise on the Court, "It would be inexpedient to take two of the Associate Judges from the same state. The practice has been to disseminate them through the United States."[15] While presidents no longer feel as constrained as Washington (both Justice O'Connor and Chief Justice Rehnquist have strong ties to Arizona, as do Justices Scalia and Ginsburg to New York), it has been historically true that in any given year the Court has represented a healthy percentage of the population (between 42.5 and 78.2 percent, depending on the calculation)—hardly a surprise if presidents view these seats as political tools.

We might say the same of religion—as when Dwight Eisenhower appointed the Catholic William J. Brennan Jr. to the Court, a result, at least in part, of direct lobbying by Cardinal Spellman. The first Catholic named to the Court was Roger Taney, who was nominated in 1835, defeated when the Senate postponed its vote indefinitely, renominated less than a year later, and finally confirmed in 1836. A second Catholic, Edward White, was not named until 1894. Since then, for all but eight years, at least one Catholic has sat on the Court. A so-called Jewish seat existed from 1916, when Louis Brandeis was confirmed, until 1969, when Abe Fortas resigned. Douglas Ginsburg, who is Jewish, was nominated by Reagan in 1987 but withdrew following allegations that he smoked marijuana with students while on the faculty of Harvard Law School. Both of President Clinton's nominees, Ruth Bader Ginsburg and Stephen Breyer, are Jewish.

That two Jewish and three Catholic (Kennedy, Scalia, and Thomas) justices now sit on the Court is telling. These days, religion (and region) has taken a back seat to race, sex, and ethnicity as vehicles for furthering partisan goals. Though presidents serving in the 1950s and 1960s contemplated some of these factors, it was Jimmy Carter who emphasized them. When Carter took office, only eight women had ever served on a federal court. Owing almost exclusively to the 144 new judgeships created by the Democratic legislature during his tenure, Carter was able to appoint 40 women to the nation's trial (29) and appellate (11) courts. He also appointed 37 black judges—nearly double the number of all his predecessors combined. To some, Carter's commitment to diversifying the federal bench reflected a genuine concern on his part about human rights. That may be true, but surely appointing women and blacks did little to damage his standing with crucial Democratic constituencies.[16]

Either way, Carter's emphasis on diversity continues today. Bill Clinton faced pressure from civil rights groups to appoint black judges, and as we shall see, his administration went to great lengths to accommodate those groups. Now in 2005, George W. Bush must be tempted to appoint Hispanics to the bench, but especially to the Supreme Court, on which no Hispanic has ever served (unless we count, as do some, Benjamin Cardozo, a Jewish justice of Spanish descent). Undoubtedly, this is a group of voters to which his party wants to appeal, in much the same way that Nixon sought out southerners and Carter courted blacks and women. What is more, if social science research demonstrating the importance of symbolic appeals, such as Bush's Spanish-speaking ability, to many constituencies, including Hispanics, is any indication, appointments to the bench may well have the desired effect.[17]

Bush has hardly missed the point. Of his 202 appointments through 2004 to the lower federal courts, 10.4 percent have gone to Hispanics, a percentage higher than any of his predecessors.[18] In addition, the names of several Hispanics appear on his list of possible Supreme Court nominees, most notably his current attorney general, Alberto Gonzales.

Appointing Hispanics to the bench may result in *future* payoffs to the Republican party, or so the current President Bush and his advisors may hope. In other cases, presidents have used the power of appointment to pay off *prior* political debts. In 1952 Earl Warren, then the governor of California, saw that his chances for obtaining the Republican presidential nomination were faltering, and so he threw his and his state's support to General Eisenhower rather than Eisenhower's rival, Senator Robert Taft of Ohio. One year later, Eisenhower nominated Governor Warren to replace Chief Justice Fred Vinson. Similarly, John F. Kennedy's friend Byron White, best known as an all-American football player, received a seat on the Supreme Court in 1962, two years after organizing Citizens for Kennedy-Johnson.

Ideological Goals

Attempting to advance electoral or partisan goals through appointments is fairly common, but it is not the only political force at work; candidates' ideology or policy values may be just as important, if not more so. Some observers assume that this is a relatively new presidential consideration, dating back only to the Reagan administration in the 1980s. This is emphatically not the case. While Reagan's advisors did care a great deal about packing the federal bench with judges and justices who shared their commitment to a particular (conservative) ideology, so too did many of their predecessors. Thomas Jefferson hoped to rid the judiciary of judges attached to a Federalist philosophy—in other words, virtually every jurist appointed by his predecessors, George Washington and John Adams. Richard Nixon may have talked about appointing strict constructionists to the bench, but according to an internal memo written by none other than William Rehnquist (then an assistant attorney general), this is what the Nixon administration meant:

> A judge who is a "strict constructionist" in constitutional matters will generally not be favorably inclined toward claims of either criminal defendants or civil rights plaintiffs—the latter two groups having been the principal beneficiaries of the Supreme Court's "broad constructionist" reading of the Constitution.[19]

The current President Bush is even more transparent, publicly equating ideology with particular approaches to constitutional interpretation: "I don't believe in liberal, activist judges," the president has said. "I believe in strict constructionists. And those are the kind of judges I will appoint."[20]

The manifestations of this emphasis on ideology are easy enough to spot. As we explained back in Chapter 1, throughout history it is the rare appointment that falls outside the president's own political party (a rough indicator of ideology), and when cross-party appointments do occur, they may well go to an ideological compatriot, such as when Nixon appointed the conservative Democrat Lewis Powell. The current President Bush is no exception. Of his 202 appointments to the district and appellate courts (through 2004), 85.6 percent have gone to Republicans, and all of those proposed as possible contenders for a seat on the Supreme Court have a noticeable connection to the Republican party.[21]

By the same token, the majority of appointments to the federal courts have engaged in what Professor Sheldon Goldman calls "past party activism"—in other words, activities designed to advance their party's interest, such as campaigning, organizing, or fund-raising.[22] Goldman's data run back to the Roosevelt years, but equally high—or even higher—levels may have existed in earlier years as well. Ulysses S. Grant (1869–1877) may himself have been "bored" by politics, but his advisors made clear to the president that he "needed to pack the [Supreme] Court with Republican loyalists." As a result, Grant "resolved at the outset that a safe Republican record would be a basic requirement for nomination, to which he added geographic suitability." "Other qualifications," Henry Abraham reports, "appeared not to matter."[23]

That a high fraction of judicial seats go to activists is not altogether surprising. Service to prominent party members may be precisely why the candidate came to the administration's attention. Service also may reveal something about the candidate's ideological commitments. Either way, the practice of rewarding loyal partisans continues today: about two out of every three Bush appointments to the circuits have been involved in party politics, as have many of those on his list of possible Supreme Court nominees (see Figure 3.1).[24] Some have even contributed to Bush's campaigns or worked on his behalf, including Michael McConnell and John G. Roberts—two names that appear on virtually all inventories of leading contenders for a spot on the high court.

Of course, we can name plenty of active Republicans who would likely not appear on any list compiled by the Bush administration. Senators Lincoln Chafee (Rhode Island), Susan Collins (Maine), Olympia Snowe (Maine), and Arlen Specter (Pennsylvania) are all Republicans, but they are all relatively liberal, what some call RINOs (Republicans in name only)—in much the same way that Lewis Powell was a conservative Democrat, a DINO of sorts.

Partisanship, it turns out, does not always neatly translate into ideological compatibility, and so presidents and their advisors must resort to other methods to ensure that candidates will meet their policy objectives. The "litmus tests" employed during the Reagan years are legendary. The president and his advisors repeatedly rejected candidates, even if they were supported by Republican senators or governors, who did not hold the administration's conservative values. Conservative appeals court judge

Anthony Kennedy, appointed to the Supreme Court in 1988, did not originally pass muster, as a close reading of his record by the Justice Department revealed a "distressing" acceptance of privacy rights. Only after the
failure of two more-conservative candidates, Robert Bork and Douglas
Ginsburg, did Reagan appoint Kennedy to the Supreme Court.[25]

But ideological screening predates that administration and, of course,
has hardly been limited to conservatives. Skirmishes with anti–New Deal
judges and justices prompted FDR to seek out nominees who shared his
policy visions. Knowing that, those proposing names for FDR's consideration were unhesitant to stress their candidate's commitment to "liberalism" and "progressive" causes. "Active opponents of the New Deal,"
Sheldon Goldman writes, "were not seriously considered." And if a doubt
existed, the Roosevelt administration scrutinized a candidate's background,
in much the same way as successor administrations now do. In the case of
a New Hampshire Supreme Court justice who was under consideration for
a position on the First Circuit, lawyers in FDR's Justice Department read
thirty-one of the justice's economic and labor decisions. When the lawyers found that the justice had ruled for the employer against an employee
in more than half, a question arose as to whether the justice was a "true
liberal." Upon further investigation, not to mention an endorsement by the
State Federation of Labor, the administration decided that the candidate
was "fit" and nominated him.[26] Clearly, the goal here was precisely the
same as it was during the Reagan years. FDR wanted to avoid "mistakes"—
judges and justices who do not share the president's political vision.

Given the screening process, we would not expect many mistakes of
this sort, and in fact they are rare, as we report in Chapter 5. But they do
occur. Kennedy's support for abortion and gay rights, not to mention his
use of foreign law in his opinions, has led Republican majority leader Tom
DeLay to label Kennedy's behavior "outrageous." The prime contemporary example of a "mistake," though, is surely David H. Souter. Prior to
his 1990 appointment to the Supreme Court, several of President George
H. W. Bush's advisors vouched for Souter's allegiance to conservative
values. But Souter's behavior on the Court has belied that promise. Souter
consistently votes with members of the Court's left wing, including John
Paul Stevens (1975–) and Clinton's two appointees, Ginsburg and Breyer.

As a result, "no more Souters" (and, more recently, "no more Kennedys")
is now a popular refrain among many conservatives, including members

of the current Bush administration.[27] And it is one that the president and his advisors have attempted to translate into action, also via extensive screening. So, for example, like his predecessors, Bush has sought to gain insight into judicial candidates by analyzing their written record. This may explain why over half of his (and his immediate predecessors') appointments have gone to individuals who had served or were serving as judges, an occupation that requires its members to write.

Of course, judicial opinions may reveal little about a candidate's ideology: the New Hampshire justice FDR considered for the First Circuit was apparently more employee-oriented than his judicial opinions let on. But in other instances the written record can be highly illuminating. Such was the case with Robert H. Bork. Undoubtedly the Reagan administration viewed Bork as the ideal justice, at least in part because as a law professor and later as a circuit court judge, he had taken conservative stances on virtually all the major social issues of the day.[28] Michael Luttig, whom George W. Bush may very well nominate to the Supreme Court, supplies another example. As a federal appellate court judge, Luttig has supported the death penalty, allowed states to require parental notification before a minor can obtain an abortion, struck down the Violence Against Women Act, and upheld a ban on partial-birth abortions. Surely in the case of Luttig (not to mention Bork) the president need not engage in idle speculation about how he would behave as a justice. It would be odd if Luttig allied himself with the Court's liberal wing. (Then again, when the Nixon appointee Harry Blackmun joined the Court in 1970, he was a regular member of its conservative camp; by the time he retired in 1994, he was an out-and-out liberal. So extreme swings are possible, if rare.)

Gaining insight into candidates' political values by scrutinizing their writings is effective, of course, only when a contemporaneous and relatively large record exists. That does not always hold, not even for sitting federal judges. A search of texts produced by John G. Roberts, another oft-mentioned contender for a seat on the Supreme Court, turns up a couple of "notes" he wrote in 1978, as a student at Harvard Law School, and several rather unilluminating pieces he penned in the 1990s, mainly for newspapers. By the same token, since ascending to the federal bench in 2003 Roberts has authored only about forty opinions. None seems particularly revealing of his views on controversial social issues of the day.

What the Roberts case suggests is that analyses of the written record do not always or even often supply presidents with the information they need to avoid "a Souter." Fully aware of this, the president's advisors subject all candidates to a vetting process, occasionally extensive. As Janice Brown, a California Supreme Court justice whom George W. Bush (unsuccessfully) sought to appoint to the federal bench in 2003 and (successfully) renominated in 2005, described it, she was interviewed by White House and Justice Department officials on three separate occasions. Brown also completed two applications for background checks, as well as questionnaires for the Justice Department and, later, the Senate.[29]

Certainly some of this screening involves matters other than ideology, but it would be surprising if the topic did not come up. At the very least, the pursuit for like-minded candidates finds some expression in the various surveys candidates complete, as the following question reveals.

> Please discuss your views on the following criticism involving "judicial activism."
>
> The role of the Federal judiciary within the Federal government, and within society generally, has become the subject of increasing controversy in recent years. It has become the target of both popular and academic criticism that alleges that the judicial branch has usurped many of the prerogatives of other branches and levels of government. Some of the characteristics of this "judicial activism" have been said to include:
>
> a. A tendency by the judiciary toward problem solution rather than grievance-resolution;
>
> b. A tendency by the judiciary to employ the individual plaintiff as a vehicle for the imposition of far-reaching orders extending to broad classes of individuals;
>
> c. A tendency by the judiciary to impose broad, affirmative duties upon governments and society;
>
> d. A tendency by the judiciary toward loosening jurisdictional requirements such as standing and ripeness; and
>
> e. A tendency by the judiciary to impose itself upon other institutions in the manner of an administrator with continuing oversight responsibilities.[30]

Given President Bush's (not to mention House majority leader Tom DeLay's [R-Tex.] and Senate majority leader Bill Frist's [R-Tenn.]) use of the term "judicial activism," it would be easy enough to add "liberal" to this list of no-nos.

These types of screening mechanisms—interviews, questionnaires, and analyses of the written record—are rather obvious manifestations of the president's interest in appointing judges and justices with the "right" values. But there are also the markers of age, race, and gender. Beginning with age, note that the majority of current candidates for the Supreme Court are under sixty; George W. Bush's appointees to the circuit courts are even younger, on average about fifty-one.[31] And Bush is hardly alone. Presidents dating back to the earliest days of the Republic have valued relative youth. John Jay was only forty-three when George Washington nominated him to serve as the first chief justice of the United States. President John Adams's initial appointee, Bushrod Washington, was just thirty-six. One hundred and fifty years later, Eisenhower named the forty-three-year-old Potter Stewart to the Supreme Court, and in 1962, Kennedy appointed Byron White, who at forty-four was just a month younger than the president himself.

Some commentators say the emphasis on youth reflects the president's interest in creating a legacy. That begs the question of what kind of legacy, however. In many instances the answer is an ideological one. When Franklin Roosevelt appointed his securities and exchange commissioner, the forty-year-old William O. Douglas, to the Supreme Court, the president knew precisely what he was doing: attempting to establish allegiance to his economic policies for decades to come.

Race and gender too may be political markers. Was it merely electoral concerns that drove both Bill Clinton and Jimmy Carter to place emphasis on appointing blacks and women to the bench? Or did they assume that blacks and women would be liberal jurists as well? We might say the same of Bush's inclination to nominate Hispanics. While it is hard to generalize about how they might vote as judges—Americans of Cuban descent, for example, are more conservative than those hailing from South America—we do know that Hispanics, as a group, are more likely to vote for Republican candidates and sometimes take more conservative stances than other minority groups. According to exit polls conducted by CNN, only 11 percent of blacks but fully 44 percent of Hispanics voted for George Bush in 2004 (representing a 9 percent increase over 2000). Likewise, Hispanics tend to support prayer in school and oppose abortion on demand and same-sex marriages.[32] How these general patterns will translate into judicial decisions remains unclear. At the very least, however, they suggest that

Bush, and more generally the Republican party, may well advance both partisan and ideological agendas via appointments to members of this group.

Constraints on the President

The current President Bush has expressed his desire to nominate very conservative individuals like Antonin Scalia and Clarence Thomas. So surely Scalia and Thomas themselves should be quite high on the administration's list of candidates to replace William H. Rehnquist as chief justice when he retires.

The fact that some men and women meet a president's goals better than others, however, does not necessarily mean that these first choices will get the nod. That is because the president is hardly an unconstrained actor; rather, when he makes nominations, he must pay heed to the Senate, and in particular the norms that senators expect him to follow. Failure to do so, as we have said, can lead to defeats for the administration in both the short and long terms.

The constraints confronting the president are several in number, though none is more important than the convention of qualifications and the norm of senatorial courtesy. The first speaks to the professional merit of the president's choices, which may affect the Senate's willingness to confirm his nominees. The second also implicates senators, specifically those from the state in which the vacancy arises.

Qualifications

Without doubt presidents have nominated unqualified, even unsavory people to serve as federal judges. We think here of the drunkard and infirm John Pickering. Then there is the case of G. Harrold Carswell, a little-known federal judge from Florida whom Richard Nixon (unsuccessfully) sought to place on the U.S. Supreme Court. Carswell's record on the bench was so deficient—he was reversed far more frequently than any other judge in his circuit—that even his supporters had a hard time justifying confirmation. About the best they could muster was the infamous defense uttered by Senator Roman Hruska (R-Neb.): "Even if [Carswell] is mediocre, there are a lot of mediocre judges and people and lawyers. They are entitled to a little representation, aren't they . . . ?"[33] That Carswell had years earlier declared his belief in the principles of "white supremacy" hardly added to his reputation. (Nor did the fact that later, in 1976, he was arrested for soliciting sex outside a public men's room.)

That these judges should not have been nominated is not altogether controversial. But many cases are far murkier. Should deficiencies in, say, professional experience, temperament, or even "people skills" render a person unsuitable for service on the federal bench? Consider Judge Roger Benitez, a sitting federal magistrate, whom George W. Bush nominated to a federal district court in California. According to the American Bar Association, "a substantial number of the judges and lawyers" reported that Judge Benitez "displays inappropriate judicial temperament with lawyers, litigants, and judicial colleagues; that all too frequently, while on the bench, Judge Benitez is arrogant, pompous, condescending, impatient, short-tempered, rude, insulting, bullying, unnecessarily mean, and altogether lacking in people skills." Based in part on these reports, the ABA deemed Benitez "not qualified" for a federal judgeship. Then there is the case of Alexander Williams, a Clinton nominee for a district court seat, whom the ABA also judged as unqualified, "primarily on concerns about his professional competence. This includes concerns over his lack of substantial trial experience, the quality of his legal writings, his lack of candor . . . and by his misstating and overstating his experience."[34]

It is just these sorts of nominees, not the easier cases of Carswell and Pickering, that prompt debate over the larger question of what actually constitutes a "qualified" candidate. But a resolution is not in the offing, at least in part because the U.S. Constitution itself does not speak to the matter. Unlike many other societies, which specify qualifications for their (constitutional) court judges (see Figure 3.2), U.S. laws are silent. One need not even be a lawyer to attain appointment to the Supreme Court, though no justice has lacked at least some training in the law.

THE IMPORTANCE OF QUALIFICATIONS

Which takes us to the chief point. Despite the lack of formal criteria, most presidents have sought to appoint persons of professional merit to the bench. This is not to say that they have necessarily and uniformly viewed a lack of qualifications as a barrier to nomination. Surely they do not, and the Carswell example illustrates as much. Even Nixon administration insiders considered him a "boob" and a "dummy." And we could say much the same of President Franklin D. Roosevelt's nomination of Richard M.

Figure 3.2
Qualifications to Serve as a Justice in Select Countries
(Of 27 European nations examined in a recent study of qualifications, only France
did not specify any for service on the highest constitutional court.)

Country	Qualifications for Appointment to the Highest (Constitutional) Court
Iceland	Has the "necessary mental and physical capacity"; has completed a legal education; has served as a judge or otherwise held a government legal office for 3 years; 35 years of age or older
India	Served as a judge for not less than 5 years; a "distinguished" jurist; a citizen of India
Italy	Served as a judge, a university professor of law, or a lawyer with at least 20 years of practice
Japan	At least 10 justices must be judges, public prosecutors, lawyers, and professors or assistant professors in legal science in universities; the rest need not be jurists
South Africa	At least 4 justices "must be persons who were judges at the time of appointment"
Spain	Served as a magistrate or prosecutor, university professor, public official, or lawyer— "all of whom must be jurists of acknowledged competence with at least 15 years of professional experience"

Duncan, a U.S. representative from Missouri. When then-Senator Harry Truman (D-Mo.) wanted FDR to name Duncan to a federal trial court, FDR's attorney general, Francis Biddle, opposed the nomination: "Almost all the lawyers who know Duncan," Biddle wrote, "consider him an inexperienced and mediocre lawyer." The president ignored his attorney general's advice and nominated Duncan, who, with Truman's backing, was easily confirmed.[35]

In this case, FDR seemed more interested in appeasing a senator than in appointing a person of merit, but for many of the president's other nominations "judicial temperament" carried the day. More generally, qualifications are of at least some concern to presidents, and have been since the George Washington administration. While the nation's first president may have been chiefly motivated to appoint loyal Federalists to the bench—

men who shared his commitment to a strong central government—from among this group he sought out candidates with judicial experience as well. Eight of Washington's ten appointees to the Supreme Court had served as state judges, and the remaining two had impressive legal credentials. William Paterson (1793–1806) had coauthored the Judiciary Act of 1789, the cornerstone of the federal legal system, and James Wilson (1789–1798) was "one of the country's most acclaimed legal scholars."[36]

Why do presidents seek out meritorious candidates, especially since the Constitution does not require them to do so? They themselves may well prefer highly qualified candidates, but another answer revolves around the Senate. As we have noted throughout, the president cannot achieve any of his goals—whether focused on advancing his partisan or policy interests—unless the Senate confirms his candidates. And senators are more likely to support the candidates they perceive as qualified for office. Again, this was true during the nation's earliest days and it remains so even today, an era in which many commentators claim that professional merit is immaterial to the Senate's deliberations and that only the candidate's ideology (relative to senators') matters.

As we shall see in the next chapter, there is some truth to this claim. But even we, who argue that the appointments process is replete with ideological and partisan considerations from beginning to end—from the creation of a vacancy on the federal bench and the president's choice of a nominee to fill it to the Senate's decision over whether to consent to the nomination— cannot belie the role of professional merit in the confirmation process. The evidence, as we lay it out in Chapter 4, is just too overwhelming.

It is thus no wonder presidents seem to take seriously a candidate's qualifications for office. Qualifications figure prominently into the Senate's calculations. But the need for approval from the Senate may not be the only reason. If the president is concerned with leaving a lasting legacy to the nation in the form of jurists who will continue to exert influence on the law well after he leaves office, then professional merit too may come into play. To be sure, some twentieth-century appointees who were thought to lack the requisite qualifications went on to be great judges; Hugo L. Black (1937–1971), a senator at the time of his appointment, provides an example. But Black may be the exception. As it turns out, many judges universally acclaimed as great by contemporary legal scholars were also universally perceived as exceedingly well qualified at the time of their nomination. We think here of the Supreme Court justices Oliver Wendell Holmes (1902–1932), Benjamin Cardozo (1932–1938), William J. Brennan, and more recently Antonin Scalia (1986–), and the circuit court judges Richard Posner (1981–) and Frank Easterbrook (1985–). In some instances, as we explain in Chapter 5, the appointing presidents would have been pleased with the legacy they left (for example, Ronald Reagan and Scalia). In others, their displeasure is a matter of public record (Dwight Eisenhower thought Brennan a "mistake"). Either way, though, it is hard to deny the effect that outstanding jurists have had on the course of American legal history, an effect that transcends their appointing president.

THE ROLE OF THE AMERICAN BAR ASSOCIATION

Whatever the reason for the emphasis on qualifications, we are still left with the question of how presidents evaluate candidates' professional merit. In earlier periods in American history, presidents often relied on their own advisors and eventually the FBI to conduct background checks on possible nominees, as well as to assess their qualifications. Attorney General Biddle's information about the "mediocre" Missouri representative Richard Duncan, for example, came in part from an FBI investigation.

FBI checks continue today but are focused more on candidates' personal background and fitness than on their professional merit. As one Justice Department official explained it:

> In this process, [FBI] agents interview Federal and state judges, attorneys, associates, government officials, business and civic leaders, religious and civil rights leaders, neighbors and [the] personal physician. National agency, police and credit checks are made. An Internal Revenue Service report is obtained.[37]

Without doubt these investigations have served to root out ethically or otherwise problematic candidates prior to nomination, but major gaffes have occurred. Nixon's counsel, John Dean, tells us that the FBI's report on the "mediocre" Carswell failed to mention either Carswell's racism or his affairs with men while he was married. This was disconcerting, as Dean explains, for while "Richard Nixon was always looking for historic firsts, nominating a homosexual to the high Court would not have been on his list."[38] Likewise, the FBI failed to unearth the fact that Douglas Ginsburg had smoked marijuana with his students. It was the press that first reported the story.

In addition to the FBI, every president since Dwight Eisenhower (with the exception of the current president, George W. Bush) has relied on the American Bar Association (ABA), through its Standing Committee on Federal Judiciary, to prescreen possible candidates. After inspecting a questionnaire completed by candidates and interviewing them and their professional colleagues, the committee produces an evaluation for each would-be nominee—"well qualified," "qualified," or "not qualified"— which it supplies to the White House. (See Figure 3.3.)[39]

Because these ratings are supposed to reflect "professional qualifications and . . . not a nominee's philosophy or ideology," at least some presidents (and senators) seem to have regarded them as something of a gold standard for evaluating a candidate's merit and have been especially loath to nominate those receiving the troublesome "not qualified."[40] Only a very small fraction—less than 1.5 percent—of all candidates nominated since Eisenhower's administration received a "not qualified" rating.[41]

Nonetheless, these data, however informative, cannot convey the occasionally manipulative and sometimes controversial relationship between the ABA and various administrations. Richard Nixon, for one, said he would not make a nomination to the Supreme Court unless the ABA cleared it, but at the same time he attempted to exploit the organization for his own purposes. When some of Nixon's advisors suggested that naming a woman to the Supreme Court would help the president with his quest for reelection, he sent Mildred Lillie's name (among others) to the ABA. Nixon apparently had no intention of nominating Lillie; he asked the ABA to evaluate her only because he believed the organization would find her, a woman and a mere state court judge, "not qualified" for service. That way he could get credit for attempting to seat a woman but, ultimately, could blame the ABA for failing to do so. And that is precisely what happened.[42]

"Steering" of sorts continues in the contemporary era. As an insider during the Clinton years tells it, when the ABA gave the administration advance notice of a "not qualified" ranking, sometimes Clinton would withdraw the name from consideration. But in other instances Clinton's advisors attempted to work with the ABA to ratchet up the ranking.[43] At the end of the day, only three of the president's 305 appointees to the district courts and none of his circuit court judges received a rating of "not qualified." But a total of thirty-five of his lower court nominees received a

Figure 3.3
ABA Standing Committee on Federal Judiciary

Membership

The Standing Committee on Federal Judiciary of the American Bar Association consists of fifteen members—two members from the Ninth Circuit, one member from each of the other twelve federal judicial circuits and one member-at-large. Appointments to the Committee are based on a reputation for the highest professional stature and integrity. The members have varied backgrounds and professional experience and are appointed for staggered three-year terms by the President of the ABA. No member serves more than two terms.

Function

The Committee evaluates the professional qualifications of persons nominated for appointment to the Supreme Court of the United States, U.S. circuit courts of appeals, U.S. district courts, the Court of Appeals for the Federal Circuit, the Court of International Trade and the territorial district courts for the Virgin Islands, Guam and the North Mariana Islands.

The Committee never proposes candidates for the federal judiciary, believing that to do so might compromise its evaluative function. Rather, its sole function is to evaluate nominees.

Evaluation Criteria

The Committee's evaluation of nominees to the federal bench is directed solely to their professional qualifications: integrity, professional competence and judicial temperament.

Integrity is self-defining. The nominee's character and general reputation in the legal community are investigated, as are his or her industry and diligence.

Professional competence encompasses such qualities as intellectual capacity, judgment, writing and analytical ability, knowledge of the law and breadth of professional experience.

In investigating judicial temperament, the Committee considers the nominee's compassion, decisiveness, open-mindedness, courtesy, patience, freedom from bias and commitment to equal justice under the law.

The Committee believes that ordinarily a nominee to the federal bench should have been admitted to the bar and engaged in the practice of law for at least twelve years. In evaluating the experience of a nominee, the Committee recognizes that opportunities for advancement in the profession for women and members of minority groups may have been limited. Substantial courtroom and trial experience (as a lawyer or a trial judge) is important for nominees to both the appel-

---

Figure 3.1 (*continued*)

late and the trial courts. Additional experience that is similar to in-court trial work—such as appearing before or serving on administrative agencies or arbitration boards, or teaching trial advocacy or other clinical law school courses—is considered by the Committee in evaluating a nominee's trial experience.

Significant evidence of distinguished accomplishment in the field of law may compensate for a nominee's lack of substantial courtroom experience.

Because an appellate judge deals primarily with records, briefs, appellate advocates and judicial colleagues (in contrast to witnesses, parties, jurors, and live testimony), the Committee may place somewhat less emphasis on the importance of trial experience as a qualification for the appellate courts. On the other hand, although scholarly qualities also are necessary for the trial courts, the Committee believes that appellate court nominees should possess an especially high degree of scholarship and academic talent and an unusual degree of overall excellence. The ability to write lucidly and persuasively, to harmonize a body of law and to give guidance to the trial courts for future cases are considered in the evaluation of nominees for the appellate courts.

While the Committee recognizes that civic activities and public service are valuable experiences for a nominee, they are not a substitute for significant experience in the practice of law in either the private or public sector.

Source: Excerpted from American Bar Association, "The Standing Committee on Federal Judiciary: What It Is and How It Works" (2005). Available at www.abanet.org/scfedjud/home.html

---

mixed rating, with a majority of the committee rating the nominee "qualified" but a minority assigning an "unqualified" rating.

Nixon's and Clinton's attempts at working with the ABA to change candidates' ratings were not public at the time. But during presidencies in between the two, the ABA was embroiled in several highly public controversies. Jimmy Carter promised to appoint women to the federal bench. At the same time, he stated that he would not send any "not qualified" nominees to Senate. These twin commitments, it turned out, were difficult to fulfill, owing at least in part to the ABA. "We had some problems," Carter's attorney general, Griffin Bell, later explained, "because we are trying to follow the ABA standard of [requiring] fifteen years' practice experience [for a rating of "qualified" or above], and many of the women didn't have fifteen years. . . . Women didn't get into law schools until the sixties." Other observers, especially leaders of civil rights groups, were less charitable, claiming that the ABA was a sexist organization that stymied Carter's efforts. After a showdown of sorts over the prospective nomination of Professor Joan Krauskopf—whom the ABA rated as unqualified because she had no trial court experience and studied the "narrow" area of family law—women's organizations lobbied Carter to bypass the ABA. An all-out war was averted when the administration pressured the organization to rethink its criteria. It also probably did not hurt that for the first time in the association's history, it appointed a woman to chair its Standing Committee on Federal Judiciary.[44]

That truce of sorts turned out to be temporary. Twenty years after Carter, in March 2001, the George W. Bush administration announced its decision to terminate the ABA committee's role in prescreening candidates. "Although the President welcomes the ABA's suggestions concerning judicial nominees," then–White House counsel Alberto Gonzales wrote to the ABA's president, "the Administration will not notify the ABA of the identity of a nominee before the nomination is submitted to the Senate and announced to the public."[45]

Why the administration took this step, as we noted back in Chapter 1, is a matter of speculation. The White House claims that it is unfair to allow one particular organization to play such a prominent role in recruiting judges when many other groups desire to participate in the process. Some commentators, though, say the move can be traced back to the Reagan years, when ABA committee members split over Judge Robert H. Bork's fitness for service on the Supreme Court. At that time, ten members viewed him as "well qualified," one voted "not opposed," and four rated him "not qualified." This vote angered some Republicans then and continued to remain a sticking point, especially in light of more recent charges that the ABA is generally biased against conservatives.[46]

To some observers these claims are the height of irony, for historically the ABA was a bedrock of reaction, founded to oppose Supreme Court decisions that legitimized governmental regulation of big business. The association was, as the great legal scholar Edward S. Corwin said, "a juristic sewing circle for mutual education in the gospel of laissez faire."[47] As late as World

War II, it largely excluded African Americans, Jews, and women from membership. But apparently, according to its critics, times have changed, and now conservatives do not get a fair hearing from the ABA.

The ABA claims otherwise, and several scholars have come to the association's aid. But it is too late for it to regain its prescreener role with the Bush administration. Whether future presidents will follow suit or revisit the Bush decision to forgo the ABA's input remains unclear.

What is true, though, is that while the ABA no longer receives advance information on judicial nominees, it continues to rate them—and, interestingly enough, by the ABA's lights George W. Bush's nominees are relatively meritorious, with 62 percent of his nominees receiving a "well qualified" rating (compared to 57 percent for Clinton's nominees).[48] Indeed, the ratings of some of his candidates have been so favorable that the (liberal) *New York Times* accused the ABA of acting as a "rubber stamp for the administration's nominees."[49] We should not take this to mean, however, that Bush, any more than his predecessors, is unwilling to name the occasional "not qualified" judge. He has, in fact, nominated four (through 2004), at least in part because they may have worked to advance other goals. We think here of state court judge Dora Irizarry, who helped New York governor George E. Pataki court Hispanic voters and whom the governor wanted to reward with an appointment to a district court in that state. While Irizarry received a "not qualified" rating from the ABA—amid allegations that she yelled at lawyers in her courtroom—Bush went ahead and nominated her anyway. She was confirmed in June 2003.[50]

What is also true is that President Bush, while removing the ABA from the prescreening process, has not hesitated to cite its ratings when they work to his advantage. In defending nominees against Senate charges of "extremism," he occasionally points to their "unanimous [ABA] rating of well qualified," as he did in the case of the (unsuccessful) nomination of Miguel Estrada to serve on a federal circuit court. Estrada, the president said, "earned the American Bar Association's highest mark . . . but [the Senate] still won't confirm him."[51]

Senatorial Courtesy

The Senate never did confirm Estrada, who ended up withdrawing from consideration. This is a fate that befalls relatively few lower federal court nominees, however. The vast majority (about four out of every five) are rather handily confirmed, at least in part because presidents have adhered to various norms within the Senate—most of which are intended to ensure that senators who are from the state where the nominee will serve (home-state senators) and who belong to the president's party have some role in filling vacancies on the lower federal bench (especially to the district courts, which do not cross state lines).

Senatorial courtesy is chief among these norms. Operative since the days of the Washington administration, courtesy holds that home-state senators of the president's party can block a nomination without supplying a reason. Should a home-state senator invoke courtesy, the nomination is usually doomed. Such was the fate of Franklin D. Roosevelt's nominee Floyd Roberts. When in 1939 Roosevelt attempted to appoint Roberts to a district court in Virginia, above the objections of the two home-state Democratic senators, one invoked courtesy. "It is my sincere and honest conviction that this nomination was made for the purpose of being personally offensive to the Virginia Senators, and it is personally obnoxious to me, as well as to my colleague." The Senate, in the face of this home-state objection, rejected Roberts by a 9–72 vote. (FDR later retaliated by refusing to nominate a senator's candidate for a position on the Third Circuit, choosing instead his friend Francis Biddle.)[52]

In this case, the Virginia senator verbalized his "courtesy" objection. More typically, senators invoke courtesy through "blue slips," which are sheets of light blue paper that the Senate's Committee on the Judiciary sends to the home-state senators, regardless of their party affiliation. The home-state senators, in turn, decide whether to support the nomination. If one or both of the home-state senators withhold their blue slips or otherwise object to the nomination, it is up to the Judiciary Committee's chair to decide whether to go forward with the nomination. When he served as chair of the Judiciary Committee during the Clinton years, Orrin Hatch's (R-Utah) practice was to allow "aggressive" use of blue slips by his fellow Republicans to block nominations made by the Democratic White House. Some say Hatch took a different approach after George W. Bush became president, declaring that "negative blue slips will be given substantial consideration . . . but they will not be dispositive unless there wasn't consultation" between the White House and the senator. In other words, while the Bush administration would "consult" with Democratic home-state senators, Hatch suggested that his committee might well ignore any objections those senators raise, and schedule hearings over the nominee.

How a chair decides to interpret senatorial courtesy can have consequences for nominations to the lower federal courts. By his own count, Hatch blocked seventeen Clinton nominees on the ground that "they lacked home state support, often because of a lack of presidential consultation with the nominee's home state senators."[53] But his interpretation had little influence on Supreme Court nominations. While in earlier eras, when region exerted a greater influence on the selection of justices, home-state senators did occasionally attempt to block nominations, these days courtesy and blue-slipping are not in much evidence over candidates to the Supreme Court. As a result, senators, though free to submit names to the administration, have little expectation of seeing their favored candidate get the nod.

On the other hand, presidents cannot ignore the Senate altogether when contemplating Supreme Court nominations. In fact, out-and-out failure to include at least some key players in the vetting process can result in trouble down the road. The 1987 Reagan administration, for example, apparently took at face value Senate Judiciary Committee chairman Joe Biden's 1986 comment that if a well-qualified conservative such as Robert Bork was nominated for the Supreme Court, he would have to support him; the president's advisors seemed to forget that Biden is, well, a politician. Hence when Reagan nominated Bork, Biden quickly lined up against him.[54]

By the same token, because the Senate has shown its willingness to reject candidates for the high court, failure to take into account its overall preferences and possible actions at the nomination stage can place a candidate at risk for rejection. Consider the political situation that President George W. Bush would likely confront if the Democrats took control of the Senate after the 2006 elections. In this case, Bush would be dealing with a Senate far more liberal than he.

Surely Bush's goals in 2006 would be the same as in 2005. He would want to move the moderately conservative Court to a more right-of-center posture, especially on key issues such as abortion, affirmative action, regulation, and gay rights. But what would happen if he attempted to appoint an ultraconservative to the bench in 2006 should his party no longer control the Senate? The Democrats might well reject that person; knowing that, Bush would probably consider nominating a candidate closer to the existing Court. That candidate would not be the president's first choice (nor, for that matter, the Senate's), but by compromising, the president and his party could avoid paying whatever political costs an unsuccessful confirmation battle might entail.

At the very least, this is the way many of his predecessors approached their task. When confronted with a hostile Senate, they have modulated their appointments, moving to the right or left as necessary. Ford's nomination of the moderate John Paul Stevens rather than the conservative Robert Bork in light of an overwhelmingly Democratic Senate is a prime example of this kind of presidential pragmatism. The Senate responded in kind, voting 98–0 to confirm Stevens. Of course, not all compromise candidates receive unanimous votes, but the inclination of most (though certainly not all) presidents to move toward the Senate may well explain why the rejection rate of Supreme Court nominees is not higher than it is.

Overcoming the Constraints

Short of appeasing senators, whether by taking into account their recommendation or their political preferences, what might a president do to work around the constraints he confronts? What strategies does he have at his disposal to see his nominees confirmed?

One is to "go public," that is, to convince Americans that his candidate is well suited for the position and that only the partisan, ideological Senate can stand in the way. Following in the footsteps of many of his predecessors, George W. Bush has attempted a form of this strategy. Throughout 2004 and into 2005, he accused Senate Democrats of "using unprecedented obstructionists tactics" to block his nominees, while simultaneously attempting to appear above politics himself: "Every judicial nominee should receive an up-or-down vote in the full Senate, no matter who is President or which party controls the Senate." "It is time," Bush said, "to move past the partisan politics of the past, and do what is right for the American legal system and the American people." At the same time, he continued to tout even seemingly doomed candidates, such as Janice Brown and Priscilla Owen, as "superb" and an "absolutely right pick for their respective positions."[55]

Sticking by his nominees turned out to be a good strategy for Bush. Owing to an eleventh-hour compromise, the Senate has now approved

Owen and Brown. But it is an indirect strategy at best. By playing to the public, Bush was lobbying citizens to contact their senators. Other presidents (and Bush as well) have attacked the problem more directly, by seeking to cut deals with legislators or, more dramatically, by maneuvering around the Senate altogether. Bill Clinton took the former route in his quest to appoint his (and Hillary Rodham Clinton's) former classmate at Yale Law School and co-chair of his California election committee, William Fletcher, to the Ninth Circuit. Hoping to change the ideological composition of the left-of-center Ninth, Senate Republicans balked at the appointment of the liberal Fletcher. They agreed to proceed only if Fletcher's mother, the also-liberal Judge Betty Fletcher, vacated her seat on the Ninth and if the president appointed a candidate suggested by Republican Senator Slade Gorton to replace her. The "throw Momma from the bench" strategy eventually worked. Clinton was able to appoint his friend William Fletcher, but only by appointing a Republican to fill the other seat.[56]

This sort of bargaining is a regular feature of the appointments game. More unusual, but hardly unknown, are attempts to work around the Senate entirely. Ulysses Grant's attorney general, Ebenezer Hoar, in an effort to create a more professional judiciary, tried to evade senatorial courtesy by refusing to give home-state senators a say in nominations. Jimmy Carter, in an attempt to diversify the bench, also tried to eliminate senatorial courtesy, this time by establishing merit commissions for the selection of appellate court judges. A decade or so later, George H. W. Bush, in retaliation for the Senate Judiciary Committee's leak to the press of Anita Hill's affidavit to the Justice Department accusing Clarence Thomas of sexual harassment, said he would restrict senators' access to FBI reports.

These efforts were not terribly successful. Senators retaliated against Grant and refused to confirm Ebenezer Hoar for a position on the Supreme Court. Carter too generated his own share of problems. He may have succeeded in diversifying the bench, but his approach led to "embarrassment and splintering in his own party," and the merit commissions he established were eventually abolished. As for Bush, when the Judiciary Committee, no longer privy to the FBI reports, decided to delay Bush's appointments until it could conduct its own investigations, the administration changed its policy. But it was too late. As the legal scholar Michael Gerhardt explains, "The delay was fatal to over two dozen subsequent judicial nominees, because the nominees' earliest opportunities for hearings would not have been until 1992 at which point the Senate slowed the process to a complete standstill pending the outcome of the presidential election."[57]

And yet presidents continue to attempt end runs around senatorial norms. Bill Clinton and the Senate were able to cut a deal over Fletcher, yet the president faced a far less hospitable legislature when it came to nominations to the Fourth Circuit. Whether for policy reasons or to appease civil rights groups, Clinton came into office quite intent on diversifying the Fourth. Covering the states of Maryland, North Carolina, South Carolina, Virginia, and West Virginia, the Fourth has the highest black population in the country, but no black judge had ever served on it. It also has a (deserved) reputation as among the most conservative circuits in the nation.

During his first term in office, Clinton tried to ameliorate the situation by nominating a black district court judge to the Fourth's "North Carolina seat." But Jesse Helms, a conservative Republican from the state, refused to return a favorable blue slip. Around the same time, the Fourth's chief justice, J. Harvie Wilkinson III, an oft-named candidate for a George W. Bush appointment to the Supreme Court, reported to Congress that the Fourth's caseload was insufficiently large to justify filling vacant positions.

Facing continuing pressure from civil rights groups, Clinton attempted to break the logjam, but with no success. So in late 1999 the administration took some rather drastic steps. First, for every vacancy on the Fourth it nominated a black candidate; second, to maneuver around Helms, it moved the "North Carolina seat" to Virginia. The Republican senator there, John Warner, agreed to cooperate with the Clinton team. Virginia's other senator, the Democrat Charles Robb, "strongly supported the goal [of diversifying the Fourth], had already recommended candidates to the White House and, in an election year, was likely to exert considerable effort to secure the nominee's confirmation."

After considering Robb's suggestions, the president settled on Roger Gregory, a lawyer from Richmond, Virginia. Clinton planned to announce the nomination in June 2000. But John Edwards—then a Democratic senator from North Carolina—almost foiled the plan when he expressed anger about losing the North Carolina seat. To appease Edwards, the administration agreed to return the seat to North Carolina when the next vacancy arose. And with that Clinton nominated Gregory.

Nonetheless, and despite Robb's and Warner's support, the Judiciary Committee, with its Republican majority, failed to schedule a hearing over Gregory's nomination. In the meantime, the administration continued to nominate more black judges, whose hearings too went unscheduled. The presidential election of 2000 was on the horizon, and so with its options and time running out, the White House decided to give Gregory a recess appointment (though it waited until after the election to do so). This meant that Gregory would become a judge on the Fourth Circuit, but only temporarily. His appointment would expire at the end of the next session of Congress unless he was renominated and confirmed by the Senate.

This was a risky strategy on the Clinton administration's part. In the first place, it was clear by December 28, 2000, the date on which the president appointed Gregory, that George W. Bush would be the next president. Thus, only if the Republican Bush as well as Robb's Republican replacement, George Allen, supported Gregory would Gregory remain on the Fourth— a big if. Second, while recess appointments are certainly not unknown— in 1789 George Washington made three to the federal district courts, and since then more than three hundred judges received their jobs in this way— they have been controversial. More to the point, they have been relatively rare in the contemporary era. No president had made one of a federal judge since Carter in 1980. Clinton had to know his opponents would roundly condemn him, and they did. Senator James Inhofe (R-Okla.) not only said he would block a life-tenured appointment for Gregory but also deemed it "outrageously inappropriate for any president to fill a federal judgeship through a recess appointment in a deliberate way to bypass the Senate." Senator Trent Lott (R-Miss.) apparently told Clinton much the same, stating that he would not support any recess appointments.

Even so, Clinton succeeded. Again, amid pressure from civil rights groups and threats from Democratic senators, Senator Allen agreed to support Gregory, though not Clinton's "political manipulation." Gregory was renominated by Bush and ultimately confirmed by the then Democratic-controlled Senate by a vote of 93–1. (True to his promise, Lott cast the sole nay vote; Inhofe abstained.)[58]

The longer term may have been less successful from the Democrats' perspective. Clinton's recess appointment of Gregory opened the door for George W. Bush to make two himself: to William H. Pryor, a supporter of greater intermingling between church and state, and to Charles S. Pickering, a controversial nominee surprisingly (and perhaps disingenuously) accused of holding racist beliefs, after the Democratic-controlled Judiciary Committee rejected them.[59] The Senate has now confirmed Pryor and Pickering has retired, but surely the entire episode only serves to shore up the adage that in politics what goes around comes around.

Or maybe not. Just as Republicans widely rebuked Clinton for trying to evade constitutional norms and processes, the Democrats have said even worse of George W. Bush. Former Senate majority leader Tom Daschle claimed, "No president had ever used a recess appointment to install a rejected nominee on to the federal bench." "These actions," Daschle continued, "not only poison the nomination process, but they strike at the heart of the principle of checks and balances that is one of the pillars of American society."[60] When Democrats counterattacked by refusing to consider any other nominees, the president agreed to refrain from making any more recess appointments in exchange for the confirmation of some his candidates.[61]

Presidents are, of course, free to nominate whomever they like to the federal courts in pursuit of whatever goals move them. But as the examples of William Fletcher, Roger Gregory, William H. Pryor, and Charles S. Pickering show, the Senate can attempt to curtail that freedom, whether through senatorial courtesy, forced bargains, or nay votes.

No president is immune, not even that Master of the Senate himself, Lyndon Johnson. When in June 1968 Chief Justice Earl Warren informed Johnson of his intent to retire from the Supreme Court, the president could have selected a replacement from among any number of confirmable candidates. But the president again decided to do exactly as he pleased. He promoted his pal Abe Fortas to chief justice and then nominated another friend, appeals court judge and former member of Congress Homer Thornberry, to the seat Fortas would vacate. But 1968 was not 1965. In the face of a mediocre showing in the New Hampshire primary, Johnson chose not to run for reelection. Both Republicans and conservative southern Democrats sensed a Republican victory in November. The liberal Warren Court, which now included Abe Fortas as part of its dominant coalition, continued to exasperate conservatives with its path-breaking decisions on civil rights and criminal procedure. Finally, details of questionable financial dealings by Fortas began to emerge. Perhaps Johnson could not have imagined that the Senate, which had bent to his will on civil rights, voting rights, and Vietnam, would deny him his choice, but deny him it did. Not only was Johnson forced to withdraw the Fortas nomination amid clear signs of defeat, but Fortas himself, the president's most trusted advisor, was later forced to resign from the Court amid talk of impeachment and even criminal prosecution.

4

Confirming Federal Judges and Justices

18th September 1987, Reagan nominee for the Supreme Court, Judge Robert Bork, testifies on the fourth day of his Supreme Court confirmation hearing in Washington, D.C. Bork was rejected by the Senate.
Photo by CNP/Getty Images

When President Ronald Reagan nominated him to the Supreme Court in July of 1987, Robert Bork was hardly an unknown political entity. As the member of the Nixon administration who fired Watergate special prosecutor Archibald Cox after the president's attorney general and deputy attorney general declined to do so, Bork had earned a place in American political history.

But not even the debacle of Watergate could have prepared Bork for what lay ahead when a Democratic-controlled Senate took up his bid for a seat on the Supreme Court. On the day of the nomination, Ted Kennedy (D-Mass.) set the tone for the campaign to follow:

> Robert Bork's America is a land in which women would be forced into back alley abortions, blacks would sit at segregated lunch counters, rogue police could break down citizens' doors in midnight raids, writers and artists could be censored at the whim of the government, and the doors of the federal courts would be shut on the fingers of millions of citizens.

Scores of liberal interest groups joined Kennedy to oppose Reagan's nominee. Planned Parenthood ran advertisements reading, "State controlled pregnancy? It's not as far fetched as it sounds. Carrying Bork's position to its logical end, states could ban or require any method of birth control, impose family quotas for population purposes, make abortion a crime, or sterilize anyone they choose." The American Civil Liberties Union even dropped its fifty-one-year-old policy of neutrality with regard to Supreme Court nominees in stating its opposition to Bork.

Opponents' allegations stemmed from Bork's published writings on and off the bench. In 1963 he declared that the proposed Civil Rights Act, which prohibited race discrimination in places of public accommodations, invoked a "principle of unsurpassed ugliness." Most of the fodder, though, came from a 1971 article in which Bork criticized Supreme Court rulings that created a right to privacy and struck down prohibitions on the use of birth control even by married couples, a position that later drew him squarely into the abortion controversy. He also argued that the equal protection clause of the Fourteenth Amendment should be limited to racial discrimination (to the exclusion, for instance, of sex discrimination) and that the First Amendment is entirely inapplicable to scientific, literary, or artistic speech.

During the hearings before the Senate's Judiciary Committee, Bork repudiated many of these views. He did not, however, recant his beliefs about the right to privacy (or, more pointedly, the lack thereof). Moreover, some deemed his newly found moderation "a confirmation conversion," which impeached his credibility without softening his right-wing image.

Public pressure on the Senate to shoot down the nomination was overwhelming. Senator John Breaux (D-La.), who was first elected in 1986, told the *New York Times* that "many Southern Democrats were elected by black votes and that his [Breaux's] black supporters were making the Bork vote a 'litmus test' issue. 'You can't vote maybe.'" Constituent pressure was so great that even John Stennis of Mississippi, onetime leader of southern segregationists, voted against Bork, as did fifty-seven of his colleagues.[1]

If Robert Bork's experience in the Senate was nothing short of a bloodbath, that of his former colleague Ruth Bader Ginsburg was a virtual "lovefest."[2] Like Bork, Ginsburg was a circuit court judge in Washington, D.C., at the time of her nomination. And like Bork, she held strong views on a range of salient issues, especially women's rights. She had written in support of a federal Equal Rights Amendment and the right to an abortion. On behalf of the American Civil Liberties Union's Women's Rights Project, she had litigated important cases before the Supreme Court. But unlike

Bork, Ginsburg sailed through the appointment process. All totaled, only fifty days elapsed between her nomination on June 14, 1993, and the Senate's vote on August 3, 1993 (compared with Bork's 115), and only three senators voted against her. While Bork was condemned as a "racist," a "flamboyant provocateur," "arrogant," and a "right-wing ideologue," Ginsburg was praised as "principled," "measured," and downright "excellent."

Why do some judicial candidates find themselves "Borked" in the Senate and others at a lovefest? The answer, quite simply, involves the goals of the senators, the ones who must confirm the nominees. Just as the president's policy and partisan objectives help account for the choices he makes, the goals of senators convey information about theirs. Primarily because senators care a great deal about retaining their position and, to lesser extents, about creating good public policy and advancing their party, they must pay heed to the various actors who can thwart their chances of reelection. These actors include interest groups, which may organize and finance their campaigns; constituents, who can choose to vote for or against them; and party leaders, who have a variety of mechanisms at their disposal to help or hinder their odds of reelection.

Surely these actors, along with the senators themselves, care about appointing qualified persons to the federal bench. Indeed, this may be a threshold consideration. But, in general, their priorities are largely political: to seat judges who will advance their ideological or partisan causes. And so these priorities must become the senators' as well if they have any hope of returning to Congress.

These forces of qualifications, partisanship, and ideology come to bear on the decisions senators make over judicial nominees. Of course, senators must decide whether to confirm the nominee, a choice of chief concern to all participants in the process. But many other decisions precede that final vote and, in fact, determine whether it will ever occur.

The Senate Judiciary Committee

After presidents decide whom they want to nominate for seats on the federal bench, they transmit the name of their candidate to the Senate. The Senate in turn refers it to its Committee on the Judiciary, one of the Senate's original standing committees (authorized in 1816).[3] Like other standing committees such as Labor or Armed Services, the Judiciary Committee's composition reflects the partisan balance in the Senate. After the Democrats gained control of 55 of the Senate's 100 seats in the 1986 election, for example, the Republican Bork faced a Judiciary Committee consisting of eight Democrats and six Republicans. Likewise, the Judiciary Committee's work is, in most ways, no different from that of any other standing committee. It reviews proposed legislation within its purview (for example, criminal law and antitrust law), and if it approves, it passes the legislation to the Senate floor for a potential vote.

The Judiciary Committee also plays an equally crucial gatekeeping role in judicial nominations, deciding whether or not to recommend a candidate to the full Senate. But that role has evolved with time. It was not until the last century or so that the Senate routinely referred judicial nominees to the committee. The committee's chair did not circulate blue slips, devices that enable home-state senators to veto a lower court nomination, until the early 1900s. And it was not until 1925 that the committee invited a nominee for the Supreme Court to testify—and then it was at the request of the candidate, Harlan Fiske Stone (1925–1941), who hoped to defend various decisions made by his law firm and that he himself had made as attorney general. Stone's strategy worked: just six senators voted against him. But it did not initiate a new practice. Only in 1950 did the Judiciary Committee begin to request that all Supreme Court nominees appear, and virtually all have done so voluntarily ever since. A final change of some consequence came under the leadership of Ted Kennedy in the late 1970s, when the committee established its own staff for investigating the backgrounds of candidates. (Now Republicans and Democrats have separate investigative staffs, which regularly consult with interest groups, in addition to conducting the usual checks.)

Scheduling Hearings

These changes have, if anything, worked to enhance the power of the committee to affect the odds of a successful nomination. Most transparent to the public is the vote it takes on judicial candidates, resulting in a (usually) favorable or (less usually) unfavorable recommendation to the full Senate. The Senate also can decide against making a recommendation or even to take no action whatsoever. Either way, its final action, or nonaction, as the case may be, tends to carry great weight with the Senate, especially over lower court nominees.

Well before that vote, though, committee members must decide when and even whether to hold hearings over the nomination. These are crucial decisions because candidates whom the committee fails to invite to appear before it are all but dead.[4] Candidates refused hearings will not receive consideration by the full Senate. The timing of the hearings may be equally as important. Interest groups and opposition-minded senators may seek to hold up proceedings before the Judiciary Committee in order to mobilize opposition, to uncover a scandal of sufficient magnitude to cause a rejection or withdrawal, or even to postpone the inevitable so that a confirmable candidate does not have an immediate impact on legal policy.[5]

Figuring prominently into the decision of whether to schedule a hearing, as we hinted in Chapter 3, is how the committee chair interprets blue slips. During most of the twentieth century, chairs generally would not move on a nominee if one or both home-state senators failed to return a positive blue slip. The nomination, in other words, would simply die. When Ted Kennedy became chair in 1979, he adopted a different policy. Henceforth, the committee would discuss all nominees, even if the home-state senator failed to return a positive blue slip. Kennedy's apparent purpose was to limit the ability of certain senators to quash women and blacks nominated by President Carter. Orrin Hatch, chair of the Judiciary Committee on and off between 1995 and 2004, seemed to play it both ways, as we mentioned in Chapter 3. During the Clinton years, he used the blue-slip procedure to allow Republicans to block the Democratic president's nominees. But when Republicans gained control of the presidency in 2000, commentators allege, Hatch changed course. As long as Democratic home-state senators had been adequately consulted by the White House, they would be unable to block nominations. According to Senator Patrick Leahy, Hatch even altered the language appearing on the blue slips themselves. During the Clinton years, the slips stated, "No further proceedings on this nominee will be scheduled until both blue slips have been returned by the nominee's home state senators." Hatch dropped that proviso.

Democrats were not amused. When Hatch put his plan into action and agreed to allow the Judiciary Committee to consider a nominee for the Ninth Circuit, Carolyn Kuhl, above the objection of one home-state senator, Barbara Boxer (D-Calif.), and later of the other, Dianne Feinstein (D-Calif.), the committee's ranking Democrat, Leahy, publicly decried the move:

[Kuhl's] appearance before this Committee, despite that clearly stated opposition, is the latest in a string of transparently partisan actions taken by
the Senate's new majority since the beginning of this Congress. In each of
these actions—each of them unprecedented—Republicans have done something they never did while in the majority from 1995 to 2001. Each pro-
vocative step, taken in tandem with the White House, has broken new ground
in politicizing the federal judiciary.[6]

Leahy's party went even further. In response to their belief that Hatch
had broken with his own recent practices regarding senatorial courtesy,
Democrats filibustered Kuhl's nomination, and to date Bush has not renominated her. Of course, had senators of Hatch's party been the ones to
raise objections to Kuhl, the nomination might well have taken a different
route to failure, as Hatch probably would not have scheduled hearings in
the first place.

In other instances, chairs have sought to kill nominations less by failing
to schedule a hearing over any one in particular than by delaying action
over a set of nominees. As the 1992 presidential election approached, committee chair Joe Biden worked to slow the committee's consideration of
George H. W. Bush's judicial nominees. Biden, of course, hoped that a
Democrat would gain control of the White House. That happened when
Clinton won the election. Just two years later, the Democrats lost control
of the Senate, and Hatch took the reins of the committee. He too attempted
to delay the process and even placed a hold on all of Clinton's nominees
during the presidential impeachment proceedings in 1998–99. Politics were
surely at work here, as were perhaps personal motivations. Some claim
that Hatch was attempting to force Clinton to nominate a "political friend,"
Ted Stewart, to a judgeship in Utah. A deal was finally struck when Clinton
agreed to nominate Stewart and Hatch agreed to move forward with the
president's other candidates.[7] But their agreement came too late to be of
much use to Clinton. While the Senate confirmed Stewart, it failed to act
on many other of Clinton's late-term nominees, most of whom never received a hearing in the Judiciary Committee.

Delays of this sort may be more common these days, but they hardly
began with Biden and Hatch. In a memo to Richard Nixon, staffer Egil
"Bud" Krogh, who later served time for a Watergate conviction, tried to
explain why the administration should nominate a more conservative nominee first when attempting to fill the two vacancies left by the departures of

John Harlan and Hugo Black. Such a strategy, Krogh wrote, would help by "denying [opponents] the *time* necessary to make a public case against a man. The longer these procedures drag out, the more difficult it is for us to get our man through." Nixon did even better, splitting the Senate's attention by nominating Lewis Powell and William Rehnquist simultaneously. Eight decades earlier, in 1888, the *New York Times* reported that the Judiciary Committee's treatment of Melville Fuller, whom Grover Cleveland had nominated as chief justice, "began [with] a rousing search into all the dark abodes of scandal and tattle, to hunt for something against the character of the President's nominee." *Harper's Weekly* observed much the same:

> The president nominated for the most important office in his gift a gentleman not generally known to the country. The immediate and unanimous testimony from the State and city in which he lived, however, was in the highest degree favorable. But party spirit on the eve of a Presidential election sought every means to discredit him. [Fuller's] whole personal, professional, and political career was searched with electric lights. Months were devoted to the scrutiny but even party spirit could find nothing substantial enough on which to base a rejection of the nomination, and it was grudgingly reported to the Senate without a recommendation.[8]

Fuller was eventually confirmed, but only after substantial scrutiny and nearly three months after his nomination.

Fuller, of course, is not the only one for whom the wait seemed nearly interminable. Senators confirmed Sandra Day O'Connor just thirty-three days after her nomination on August 19, 1981, but as we have noted, for Bork the process that ended in his rejection took nearly four months, and senators did not vote on Clarence Thomas until 107 days after George H. W. Bush had nominated him.

Similar variation, it is worth noting, holds for the lower courts. While the Senate took only seven days to confirm Kenneth Starr, who later served as special prosecutor investigating Clinton, to the court of appeals in 1983, over a year went by before senators agreed to the appointment of the Clinton nominee Richard Paez. Then there is the odd case of John G. Roberts. Originally nominated by George H. W. Bush in 1991 to the U.S. Court of Appeals for the District of Columbia, considered second only to the Supreme Court in terms of its legal importance, Roberts never received a hearing. The current President Bush renominated him in 2001, but once again the committee chose not to schedule a hearing. Finally, after yet a third nomination, the committee took up Roberts's candidacy on January 29, 2003, and again on April 30, 2003. Perhaps owing to objections registered by several interest groups over Roberts's allegedly conservative positions on abortion and the environment, not to mention other controversial candidates considered on the same day, the hearing was a near marathon, starting at 9:30 a.m. and lasting until about 9 p.m. Even after the proceedings concluded, committee members continued to pepper Roberts with (written) questions. The Senate did eventually confirm Roberts—eleven years after his first nomination.[9]

Holding Hearings

Still, we hasten to note, the Robertses, Paezes, and Thomases are the exceptions, not the rule. Since the Truman presidency, chairs have scheduled, and relatively promptly at that, hearings for most of the candidates—about 85 percent. Even now, and despite accusations to the contrary, the vast majority of President Bush's nominees have had their day before the Judiciary Committee.

What is more, for most judicial offices, the hearing is not of the intense sort the nation witnessed over Robert Bork. Hearings, when they do occur, are generally brief, low-key affairs, with few witnesses testifying and very limited (if any) press coverage. No more than one out of every five nominations to the lower courts over the last five decades has generated objections of any type, whether from interest groups or others, and this figure has not increased markedly with time.[10] Even seemingly controversial nominees tend to draw little notice. Though John Roberts's candidacy dragged on, it attracted virtually no media attention. Between 2001 and 2003 the *New York Times* published precisely five stories mentioning the Roberts nomination, and then as just one of several Bush circuit court nominations. Not one article covered any questions he received or answers he gave during the proceedings.

The circumstances surrounding hearings over Supreme Court nominations are different. Given the importance of the Court, the lack of senatorial courtesy, and the relative rarity of vacancies on it, media attention is more intense. For the same reasons, interest group participation too can be extensive and senators' questioning of the nominees far more searching.

While the media are not always silent over nominees to the lower courts—the *Times* did, in fact, report on the committee's interrogation of

Jeffrey Sutton, whom it considered on the same day it took up Roberts—it rarely neglects candidates for the U.S. Supreme Court. Even from the earliest days of the Republic, the press reported on candidates to the federal bench, mostly to the Supreme Court, and, crucially, took stands on their candidacies. As Professor Richard Davis puts it, "Long before Robert Bork, press coverage had harmed a nominee's chances of confirmation." Take the case of Alexander Wolcott, whom James Madison unsuccessfully attempted to appoint to the Supreme Court in 1811. Several forces probably contributed to Wolcott's defeat, but it could not have helped his cause that newspapers in New England "panned" him. One even said that Wolcott was "more fit by far to be arraigned at the bar than to sit as a judge." A century later, Louis Brandeis (1916–1939) was the target of press attacks from the *Wall Street Journal* and the *New York Times,* among others, which deemed him a dangerous "radical." In the 1930s, it was then-Senator Hugo Black's turn. After Roosevelt nominated him, the *Washington Post* quipped that if Black "has ever shown himself exceptionally qualified in either the knowledge or the temperament essential for the exercise of the highest judicial function, the occasion escapes recollection."[11]

Even so, press coverage of Supreme Court proceedings has without doubt escalated over the last two decades. Between the time of Ruth Bader Ginsburg's nomination on June 14, 1993, and her confirmation on August 3, 1993, the *New York Times* ran forty-two more stories on her than it did in 1962 about her predecessor, Byron White, or about eight times the number it published on John G. Roberts's odyssey in the Senate.[12] Snippets of Ginsburg's speeches appeared in the newspapers, as did excerpts from her confirmation hearings, which were broadcast on television. Virtually no aspect of Ginsburg's life went unexamined. From coverage in the *Times*, we learned about her summers at Camp Che-Na-Wah in the Adirondacks, her stint as a baton twirler for James Madison High School in Brooklyn, her marriage to Martin Ginsburg, and the hospitalization of her son, at age two, after he drank Drano. We also learned what the *Times* thought of her candidacy:

> The bridge she builds to justices like John Harlan, who served from 1957 to 1971, is a reminder of the mediocrity of so many appointees of the Bush-Reagan years. Nominees chosen for ideology, or with sparse credentials out of political necessity, by increments have depressed the Court's performance,

professional standing and fidelity to law. President Clinton's nominee brings
a touch of class to the Supreme Court.[13]

The liberal-leaning *Times* is not always so complimentary. Its editors were
entirely unimpressed with Clarence Thomas's qualifications for service:

> Believe him or not, nothing in this bizarre episode [concerning Anita Hill's
> allegations of sexual harassment] enhances Judge Thomas's qualifications,
> which were slim to start. Believe him or not, his behavior on the witness
> stand does nothing to enhance those qualifications. Believe him or not, to
> confirm him is to gamble.
>
> If Judge Thomas were a brilliant jurist, a Holmes or a Brandeis, the gamble
> might be justified. But Clarence Thomas offers no such brilliance, no basis
> for gambling with the public's confidence in, and the future of, American
> law.[14]

Some say increased press attention to judicial nominees has led to a
more politicized environment surrounding the Judiciary Committee's deliberations, not to mention those of the full Senate. Does that mean that
senators' decisions over nominees are dramatically more political in response? We do not think so. Ideology and partisanship, as well as qualifications, have always figured prominently in the senators' votes over
Supreme Court nominees, as we shall explore momentarily. What has
changed, obviously, is the amount of information that the public receives
about nominees. These days, by the time the Senate must vote over any
nominee to the Supreme Court, Americans have read scores of newspaper
articles or watched any number of news programs reporting on the nomination. Information garnered from those sources undoubtedly has made
for a public more interested in the proceedings and perhaps more willing
to express its opinions to senators.

Intense press coverage, though, is not the only feature that distinguishes
Supreme Court proceedings from those over lower court nominees, nor
are the media the only source of public information about would-be justices. Interest groups, whether in support or opposition, also weigh in at
these hearings and have for a century or more. As far back as 1881, groups
opposing monopolistic railroad practices sought to block the appointment
of Justice Stanley Matthews (1881–1889), whom they thought would be
"the decisive vote in striking down legislation regulating railroads."[15] In
the 1930s, labor and civil rights groups sent telegram after telegram to

senators urging them to vote against President Hoover's choice for the Supreme Court, John Parker.

Richard Nixon's nomination of Clement Haynsworth in 1969 also generated substantial opposition. While at first it appeared that he would easily attain confirmation, confidence in Haynsworth began to erode when the Judiciary Committee unearthed cases he had decided as a lower court judge in which he had a direct financial interest. Even though Haynsworth gained but a few dollars from these transactions, his behavior made him an easy target—especially since he had been nominated to restore high ethical standards that were lacking in Fortas, who resigned under a cloud of suspected financial improprieties. On the ideological front, liberals alleged that Haynsworth had compiled an anti-union, anti-civil-rights record as an appellate judge. They pointed to his rulings holding that businesses could shut down specific factories solely for the purpose of punishing union activity, allowing private hospitals receiving federal funds to discriminate on the basis of race, and upholding "freedom of choice" school plans under which students could choose the schools they would attend, with the inevitable result that the schools remained segregated. Liberal opposition to Haynsworth produced vigorous lobbying, and, ultimately and against all initial expectations, the Senate rejected Haynsworth by a vote of 55 to 45. According to Nixon aide John Ehrlichman, the vote was a direct product of the "highly expert, expensive and intensive lobbying campaign by organized labor and civil rights groups."[16]

Since the Haynsworth nomination, interest groups have become an even more regularized part of the process, as we show in Figure 4.1, with virtually no contemporary nominee escaping their scrutiny. Few, however, were damaged more than Robert Bork. Before the Senate Judiciary Committee, seventeen groups testified against him, and even that figure is "a pale reflection of the extraordinary effort" mounted by liberals and Democrats in and outside the Senate. During the proceedings, many groups ran ads in newspapers, sent mailings to their members, and more generally launched an all-out (and expensive) attack on the candidate. Other groups made similar efforts in his defense. All campaigned vigorously with the goal of seeking to influence senators and, crucially, their constituents.[17]

Owing to limited resources, these groups cannot and in fact do not mount such intensive campaigns for and against most lower court nominations.

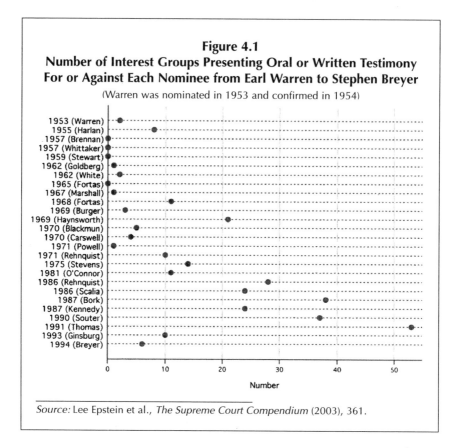

Figure 4.1
Number of Interest Groups Presenting Oral or Written Testimony For or Against Each Nominee from Earl Warren to Stephen Breyer
(Warren was nominated in 1953 and confirmed in 1954)

Source: Lee Epstein et al., *The Supreme Court Compendium* (2003), 361.

This is not to suggest that they are entirely silent. These days, groups on the right and left are only too willing to deploy their Web sites to provide the public with their views on judicial candidates. Moreover, when they do activate—whether because they think the seat is particularly important or because the nominee is especially offensive to their interests—they may have a substantial effect on the course of the nomination, perhaps convincing members of the Judiciary Committee to delay or even attempt to block it.[18] But interest group participation in proceedings over lower court nominees tends to be rather selective and sparse relative to activity concerning candidates for the Supreme Court.

Likewise, the Judiciary Committee itself tends to take its screening role far more seriously over Supreme Court nominees than over candidates for most other courts, with interrogations into the candidate's background, credentials, and philosophy deeper and more intense. Sometimes its efforts to tease out a candidate's ideology work to great effect. Robert Bork, for one, was quite willing to answer questions about his views—perhaps unavoidably so, since he had criticized certain Supreme Court decisions in such strong terms that he could not avoid telling senators under oath what he had repeatedly told the rest of the world in articles and speeches.

These days, however, most candidates are less forthcoming. Clarence Thomas not only refused to state where he stood on abortion but even tried to suggest that he had never really thought about the issue. Ruth Bader Ginsburg and later Stephen Breyer too were "strategically silent" about any issue that might come before the Court. After Ginsburg told the Judiciary Committee that "a person's birth status . . . should not enter into the way that person is treated," one member asked her about her attitude toward "sexual orientation." Her response was entirely noncommittal: "Senator, you know that that is a burning question that at this very moment is going to be before the Court. . . . I cannot say one word on that subject that would not violate what I said had to be my rule about no hints, no forecasts, no previews."[19] Such silence, while frustrating to some senators, can serve to keep nominees out of political trouble. Had Thomas stated his views on abortion, he instantly would have alienated half the Senate. As it was, he had enough trouble on his hands, owing first to questions about his qualifications and then to charges of sexual harassment. Concerns about his political views only would have added to his problems, and Thomas rather transparently avoided raising them.

The Full Senate

Whether lovefests or bloodbaths, once the Judiciary Committee has held hearings and reviewed the record, there is yet one final veto its members can exercise. A refusal to endorse a nomination is tantamount to killing it, for without the committee's endorsement the full Senate may not even consider it, much less support it. Such was the fate of President George W. Bush's nominee Charles Pickering. After the committee, then effectively controlled by Democrats, rejected Pickering, the nomination was all but dead. Even Pickering's leading supporter, Trent Lott, could not revive it. Only by doing an end run around the Senate and making a recess appointment was Bush able to place Pickering on the federal bench. Robert Bork too suffered at the hands of the Judiciary Committee. After nine of the fourteen committee members voted against him, even White House officials did not believe they could rescue the nomination.[20] They were right. Though the full Senate did take up the nomination, Bork received only forty-two yea votes. Ruth Bader Ginsburg, on the other hand, attained the unanimous endorsement of the Senate Judiciary Committee and wound up confirmed by a vote of 96–3.

Of course, senators need not accept the committee's recommendation. They can cast votes in favor of nominees the committee rejects, as forty-two did in the case of Bork. They can also cast votes against candidates the committee endorses, as three did in the case of Ruth Bader Ginsburg.

But nay votes are not the only ways senators can express their displeasure with a nomination. They also can attempt to filibuster it, that is, prevent a vote by indefinitely extending debate. Filibusters do not necessarily kill a nomination, but they may be difficult to overcome. Unless senators favoring the candidate can attain the sixty votes necessary to shut down debate (i.e., invoke cloture), the nomination dies.

Mustering those votes can be difficult, and that is why Republicans these days have called for use of the so-called nuclear option, which would eliminate filibusters over judicial nominations by requiring a final Senate vote on all nominees who receive a positive recommendation from the Judiciary Committee. But in 1968 it was the Republicans, joined by southern Democrats, were quite willing to deploy the filibuster to prevent Lyndon Johnson from promoting his friend Abe Fortas to chief justice.

Short of filibustering a nomination, senators can place a hold on it. Holds occur when a senator asks his or her party leader to delay action on a nominee; it is then up to the party leader to grant the request and to determine the length of the delay. Sometimes holds are preludes to a filibuster, but in many instances they have little to do with particular nominees. So, for example, in 1987 two Democrats, Howard Metzenbaum of Ohio and Ted Kennedy of Massachusetts, put a hold on six lower court nominees in an effort to force the Justice Department to release documents about an ambassador's possible financial lapses. Fifteen years later, in 2002, John McCain (R-Ariz.) held up judicial candidates in order to "convince" President Bush to nominate a candidate of his own choosing to the Federal Election Commission.[21]

Senators' Goals and Their Implications for Nominees

However effective they may be, holds and filibusters are relatively rare events. To date only one Supreme Court nominee, Justice Fortas, has ever been filibustered. The attempts on the part of Democrats to filibuster a handful of Bush appeals court nominees are largely unprecedented. Moreover, despite all the recent political rhetoric and commentary, most nominees make out just fine on the floor of the Senate. Of the 147 nominees to the Supreme Court on whom the Senate has deliberated since 1789, 120 (82 percent) have been confirmed.

As for lower court confirmations, some presidents have had less success with the Senate than others. On average, over 80 percent attain confirmation (see Figure 4.2). Moreover, even during the George W. Bush

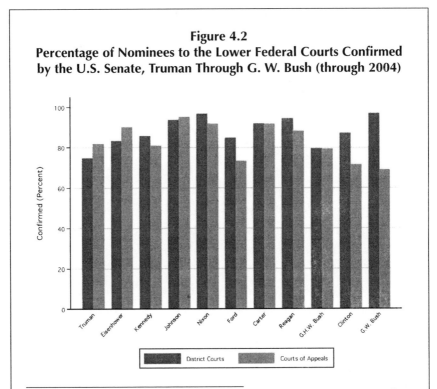

Figure 4.2
Percentage of Nominees to the Lower Federal Courts Confirmed by the U.S. Senate, Truman Through G. W. Bush (through 2004)

Sources: Mitchel A. Sollenberger, "Judicial Nomination Statistics: U.S. District and Circuit Courts, 1945–1976," Congressional Research Service, RL32122, October 22, 2003, Table 3; Denis Steven Rutkus and Mitchel A. Sollenberger, "Judicial Nomination Statistics: U.S. District and Circuit Courts, 1977–2003," Congressional Research Service, RL31635, February 23, 2004, Table 2(b); and the Web site of the Senate Judiciary Committee (http://judiciary.senate.gov/nominations.cfm).

years, the vast majority of nominees that survived the Judiciary Committee ultimately succeeded. Through the end of the president's first term, the Senate considered 224 of his judicial candidates and confirmed all but 22 (or about 90 percent).

That the Senate rolls out the welcome mat for most judicial nominees—typically, no fewer than two out of every three—is not much of a surprise in light of senatorial courtesy and, more generally, presidential consideration of the preferences of the Senate prior to nomination. But, again, most is not *all*. Reagan's attempt to appoint Bork and Johnson's to promote Fortas make that clear enough, as does John Tyler's effort, more than a hundred years earlier, to put Edward King on the Supreme Court. Tyler, who had assumed the presidency upon William Henry Harrison's death, was extremely unpopular in the Senate. That body killed the King nomination by voting to postpone action on it. Six months later Tyler tried again, and once again the Senate refused to confirm King. Before Tyler's term ended, the Senate rejected a total of five of his nominees to the Court.[22] In more contemporary times, Bill Clinton's appointees to the Supreme Court, Ginsburg and Breyer, faced little opposition in the Senate, but not so some of his nominees to the lower courts. Even more recently, George W. Bush's candidates became sufficiently controversial to raise the possibility of defeat in the Senate.

These divergent outcomes—from Ruth Bader Ginsburg's breeze through the Senate to Fortas's failure to overcome a filibuster to King's double drubbing—return us to the questions we asked at the outset: Why is it that senators attempt to filibuster some nominees but not the vast majority of them? Why do they confirm most nominees but not all? More generally, what explains the choices senators make?

The answers to these questions, we believe, lie in the motivations of legislators. According to many social science accounts of Congress, legislators are "single-minded seekers of reelection."[23] This may overstate the case; senators also are concerned with creating good public policy. But at least since passage of the Seventeenth Amendment, which provided for the popular election of senators, legislators cannot afford to systematically and regularly antagonize their constituents.

When it comes to lower court nominees, there is little risk of alienating voters. Constituents may have some opinion on features of the process; for example, 2005 polls show that about 90 percent of Americans have formed a judgment about the use of filibusters.[24] Yet most voters are unable to name any lower court nominees, much less be able to offer an assessment of them. Candidates for the Supreme Court present a much different picture. Even before the advent of modern-day polling, as we suggested above, newspapers provided information to the public about the qualifications and politics of nominees for the high court. Americans used this information to formulate their own opinions, which they in turn occasionally passed on to senators. When, in 1930, the Senate rejected John Parker for a seat on the Supreme Court, a disappointed President Hoover declared that "public opinion as a whole cannot function in this manner."[25]

Now, of course, senators need not guess about the public's views. With each Supreme Court nomination, they are inundated with survey data alerting them to their constituents' thinking. Even relatively uncontroversial, nearly invisible nominations do not escape the pollsters or, for that matter, organized interests. At the time Bill Clinton announced his intention to appoint Stephen Breyer to the Court, the Senate learned that 52 percent of Americans thought it should confirm him (37 percent had no opinion yet) and that among those who were able to voice a view, most thought Breyer was qualified for service.[26]

Senators hoping to be reelected ignore these perceptions at their own peril. At the same time, they can hardly afford to estrange other actors who can foil their chances of reelection. Organized interests are certainly among them. Despite claims that interest groups "play a small role in the appointment process and ought not be of great interest," senators must pay some attention to these groups—the very groups who help organize and finance their campaigns—or else pay a potentially high price at election time.[27] Or so some groups threaten. When leaders of the National Organization for Women were asked what they would have done had they known that Joe Biden would vote for a candidate they opposed, one was blunt: "We would have had every Delaware donor of Joe Biden on an airplane, and they would've been standing in his office. . . . We could've gone that far, and we would have. We'd get on the phone with our allies saying 'we just heard that Joe Biden is about to vote yes on this nomination.'"[28] Senators, of course, hardly miss the possible electoral consequences of crossing important organizations. As one said: "If an interest group says 'this is a key vote, we're watching this vote,' then the easy thing to do is to vote the way the group wants." Another concurred: "My colleagues who have announced their intention to seek reelection are often more sensitive to these interest groups and pay close attention to the messages of these groups."[29]

Equally as crucial to senators are their party leaders, including the president himself. In light of senatorial courtesy, we would not anticipate much opposition from same-party senators, at least not for nominees to the lower courts. But even for candidates to the Supreme Court, senators may be especially unwilling to block those nominated by a president of their own political party. To do so would be to raise the ire of party leaders, not to mention that of the president himself, to the detriment of their campaigns for reelection.

The public, interest groups, and party leaders may have distinct goals, and goals that may occasionally collide at that. Nonetheless, these actors' priorities tend to coalesce around two crucial factors: candidates' qualifications for office and their politics, in the form of partisanship and ideology. Since these are the concerns of senators' key constituencies, they must become the concerns of reelection-seeking senators as well. And, in fact, they do. As we explain below, candidates' credentials for service on the bench and their politics largely account for the choices senators make over judicial nominees.

QUALIFICATIONS

Among the more commonly held views about today's appointments process is that it is dominated by a candidate's ideology and partisanship rather than his or her competence and integrity. We do not dispute the idea that politics plays a large role—indeed, virtually everything we have written so far suggests that politics is a crucial feature of the process. On the other hand, there are good reasons to suspect that professional qualifications are hardly trivial.

In Chapter 3 we explained why presidents cannot help concerning themselves with a nominee's professional merit, and much the same holds for senators as well. In the first place, senators, while primarily interested in reelection, are not disinterested in creating good public policy. Packing the courts with unqualified persons will not well serve that goal. Nor will it help them to meet their chief objective, maintaining their seat in the Senate, since candidates' credentials may be important to key constituencies: the public and organized interests. Whether from newspaper editorials or interest group reports, Americans do form perceptions about the qualifications of nominees to the federal bench, especially to the Supreme Court, and those perceptions may affect their opinion on whether their senators should vote to confirm or not. Organized groups too ought to care about a nominee's credentials. If the goal of interest groups is to achieve the confirmation of nominees who will work to advance their policy interests once they become judges, then the better the candidate, the more influential she or he is likely to be. This may be especially true on collegial courts, on which judges sit together to make decisions.

As it turns out, this is not mere hypothesizing or wishful thinking on our part. Again, and despite all the contemporary rhetoric, qualifications do play a crucial role in the confirmation process. We learned this by gathering the votes cast by every senator over every Supreme Court nominee since the mid-twentieth century—a total of 2,451 votes.[30] We then used newspaper editorials to analyze the extent to which a nominee's qualifications influence those votes (see Figure 4.3 for an explanation of our method).[31]

On this basis, Ginsburg received the highest rating on our scale of professional qualifications (see Figure 4.4), as did seven other justices (including William J. Brennan, Lewis F. Powell, and Antonin Scalia). Thomas was on the lower end of our scale, but it was G. Harrold Carswell— reckoned "mediocre" even by supporters—whom the editors deemed the least qualified of all contemporary nominees.

To what extent are these assessments associated with Senate voting? Quite strongly, as it turns out. As we show in Figure 4.5, which depicts the percentage of votes cast by senators over highly qualified, qualified, and not qualified candidates, senators almost always vote for candidates perceived as highly qualified but are far more suspect of those with lower merit.[32] If all one hundred senators cast a vote, a highly qualified nominee would receive about forty-five more votes (on average) than one universally deemed unqualified. This may well explain why certain nominees who were very liberal (e.g., William J. Brennan) or very conservative (e.g., Antonin Scalia) sailed through the Senate. Despite their political outlooks, they received the highest possible merit rating, and senators, even those on the other side of the ideological fence, may have found it difficult to justify voting against them.

Figure 4.3
Assessing the Qualifications of Supreme Court Nominees

To what extent does a Supreme Court nominee's qualifications, relative to other factors such as the nominee's ideology or party affiliation, affect the votes cast by senators? Addressing this question requires us to develop a way to measure the extent to which a candidate is qualified to serve on the high Court. This is no simple task, as scholars and policy makers alike disagree over the characteristics that make for a "qualified" nominee; indeed, some observers argue that qualifications have always been defined politically and always will be. So, for example, to the conservative senator Orrin Hatch (R-Utah) Robert Bork was quite qualified for a seat on the Supreme Court but to the liberal Ted Kennedy (D-Mass.) he was not.

We cannot say we disagree but devising a measure of merit based on senators' (or even scholars') colored definitions of merit is not our project. Rather, our goal is to tap into the senators'—or, more precisely, assuming that senators are oriented toward reelection, their constituents'—*perceptions* of whether a candidate is qualified or not. This requires us to locate a measure of qualifications from sources external to and independent of the Senate (and, of course, that is available prior to its vote). In other words, we would not want to use a measure based on either Ted Kennedy's or Orrin Hatch's opinion of Robert Bork's (or any other nominee's) professional qualifications.

The measure of qualifications we use here was developed by one of the authors of this book, Jeffrey A. Segal, along with Albert D. Cover, and consists of an analysis of newspaper editorials written from the time of nomination by the president until the vote by the Senate. Specifically, Segal and colleagues selected four of the nation's leading newspapers, two with a liberal outlook (the *New York Times* and the *Washington Post*) and two on the more conservative end (the *Chicago Tribune* and the *Los Angeles Times*) for the years 1953–1994 and identified every editorial that offered an opinion on the candidate's qualifications. With the editorials in hand, Segal and his colleagues evaluated their content on the basis of claims about the nominee's acceptability from a professional standpoint. For example, the *New York Times* editorial about Ruth Bader Ginsburg, which we cite in the text, would be evaluated as a positive statement about Ginsburg; the editorial about Thomas would be a negative statement. After examining all the editorials, Segal and Cover then created a scale of qualifications for each nominee that ranges from +1 (most qualified) to –1 (least qualified).

As we show in Figure 4.4, the qualifications measure devised by Segal and Cover generally comports with our existing knowledge of the nominees. Note, for example, that it is Carswell—reckoned "mediocre" even by supporters—who receives the lowest score, while it is Kennedy, Ginsburg, Scalia, and several others—candidates who even would-be opponents admitted were qualified to serve—who received the highest.

Figure 4.3 (*continued*)

That the qualification scores square with our impressions of the nominees is not their only virtue. At least three others come to mind. First, the scores are external to the Senate—it is newspaper editors and not senators from whom we derived the scores—and are available and observable prior to the Senate's vote. Second, to the extent that different scholars examining the same set of editorials reach the same judgment about them, the scores seem reliable. Finally, and perhaps not so stunningly given the range of newspapers consulted, the scores are not biased by the ideology or political party of the nominee; neither liberals nor Democrats receive higher (or lower) ratings based solely on their policy preferences or partisanship. On the other side, at least one commentator has critiqued our approach to studying qualifications on the ground that qualifications and ideology are not static, instead fluctuating in response to political currents. But because the approach is indeed dynamic in this way—it is derived from editorials contemporaneous with the nomination—this is actually yet another benefit of, rather than a fatal flaw in, our approach to assessing a candidate's qualifications.

Source: Charles D. Cameron, Albert D. Cover, and Jeffrey A. Segal, "Senate Voting on Supreme Court Nominees: A Neo-Institutional Model," 84 *American Political Science Review* 525 (1990).

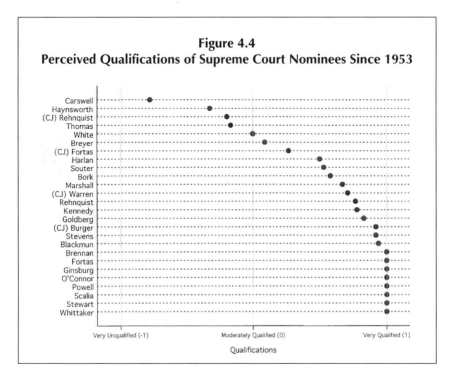

Figure 4.4
Perceived Qualifications of Supreme Court Nominees Since 1953

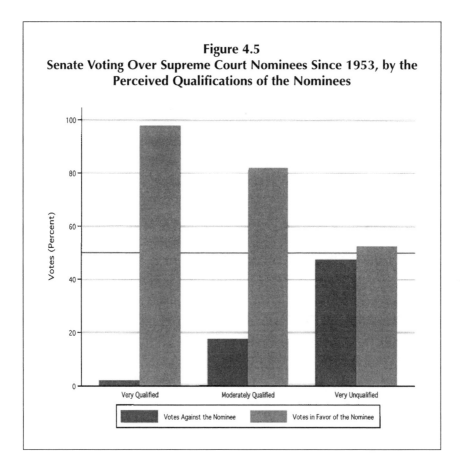

Figure 4.5
Senate Voting Over Supreme Court Nominees Since 1953, by the Perceived Qualifications of the Nominees

Of course, this is not to say that the president always taps the most capable, best qualified, or most meritorious person at any given time to fill any given vacancy. It is surely possible that there was someone in 1969 more qualified than Warren Burger to serve as chief justice or more meritorious than was Stephen Breyer in 1994, for example. But we do argue that qualifications do not appear to play as minimal a role in the confirmation of justices as some have suggested.

POLITICS

Even so, it is not simply a candidate's merit that affects the chances of a successful appointment. The partisan climate surrounding the Senate's deliberations and the candidate's ideology also play roles, and critical ones at that.

PARTISANSHIP

We already have seen that party politics figures prominently in the decisions of the Judiciary Committee. We doubt that Joe Biden, when he served as chair of the committee, would have delayed consideration of George H. W. Bush's nominees had he and the president shared a partisan affiliation. Likewise, it would be hard to imagine Democrats blocking candidates proposed by Bill Clinton, as they have done with some of George W. Bush's candidates. More systematic data, it is worth noting, shore up these stories. In a study of delay in the Senate confirmation of candidates to the Courts of Appeals, political scientists Sarah A. Binder and Forrest Maltzman find that divided government is a major culprit. When the Senate's majority is of a different party than the president, Binder and Maltzman tell us, the majority "takes advantage of its scheduling power to delay confirmation."[33] In light of their findings, it should come as no surprise that Kenneth Starr, confirmed by the Senate just a week after Reagan nominated him, had such an easy time of it. At that point, Republicans controlled both the presidency and a majority in the Senate. Equally as explicable is the 408-day gap between the time of Bill Clinton's nomination of Richard A. Paez on January 26, 1999, and Paez's confirmation on March 14, 2000, as Republicans once again had a majority in the Senate.

When it comes to Supreme Court nominees, party affiliation continues to play an important role. Senators of the same party as the president overwhelmingly support his nominees, with 94 percent of their votes, while senators of the opposition party are far more reluctant to do so, weighing in with support only 76 percent of the time. Similarly, through the history of the Republic, the Senate has confirmed just 59 percent of Supreme Court nominees under divided government (23 of 39), compared with 90 percent when the president's party controlled the Senate (97 of 108).

Then again, partisanship does not tell the whole story. The Senate confirmed the well-qualified Ronald Reagan nominee Antonin Scalia by a vote of 98–0, even though Democrats held forty-seven seats at the time. Similarly, only three of the forty-four Republicans in the Senate in 1993 voted against Bill Clinton's equally well-qualified candidate Ruth Bader Ginsburg.

For these nominees and others throughout history, congruity between the president's party and those of senators may have been less a factor than the nominees' professional merit, or even the political world surround-ing the confirmations—especially the status of the most important player in that world, the president. Certainly, senators and the public expect presi-dents to use their influence to secure a successful nomination, as Reagan did with William Rehnquist, but the fact is that the president's ability to do so depends in some measure on his own political (mis)fortunes. Surely it hurts the president when his party is the minority in the Senate, but equally problematic may be when he is in his last year in office and thus likely to have only a minimal influence over senators of either party. President Johnson found himself in this situation when he attempted to appoint Fortas to the chief justice position, and it is certainly not a position of strength. Historically, the Senate has confirmed only 56 percent of Supreme Court nominees (14 of 25) in the fourth year of a president's term, versus 87 percent in the first three years (106 of 122).

Then there is the matter of the president's popularity with the public. One would presume that higher approval ratings serve him well with the electorally minded Senate, and this is typically the case. While no one-to-one relationship between presidential approval and confirmation approval exists—President Nixon, for instance, was at the height of his popularity when the Senate rejected two of his nominees (Clement Haynsworth and G. Harrold Carswell), and President Johnson's approval rating was only at 39 percent when Thurgood Marshall was confirmed—presidents with high approval ratings (greater than 70 percent) are, on average, able to attract 98 percent of senators' votes for their candidates, while unpopu-lar presidents (approval ratings less than 50 percent) average less than 80 percent. All in all, an out-of-favor president can cost his nominee nearly 20 votes.

IDEOLOGY

Politics, in the form of ideology, also can hinder or enhance a nominee's chance of Senate approval. And, like partisanship, it can play out in differ-ent ways. One way centers less on the nominee him- or herself than on the nature of the vacancy. Maltzman and Binder show that divided govern-ment has a strong effect on the course of lower court confirmation pro-ceedings, but their study also indicates the importance of a critical nomination. Simply stated, when an appointee is likely to tip the ideological balance of a circuit, senators are more likely to drag their feet over the confirmation. This is especially so if they think the circuit is influential, as is the U.S. Court of Appeals for the Ninth Circuit. Binder and Maltzman find that the Senate took twice as long to process Clinton's nominees to the Ninth than it did for all his other appointees (five months versus ten months). Conservatives in the Senate, they say, believed that "confirming Clinton nominees [to the Ninth] would have squandered a potential opportunity to reverse the liberal tilt of a precariously balanced court."[34]

We can say much the same of seats on the Supreme Court. Scalia's qualifications for service were not the only reason he breezed through the Senate. Another was that senators perceived his appointment as being of little consequence to the composition of the Court. The conservative Scalia was to replace the equally conservative William H. Rehnquist, whom Reagan promoted to chief justice. If, on the other hand, Scalia (rather than Robert H. Bork) had been nominated to replace Lewis F. Powell, largely considered the Court's center at the time, then the lovefest might well have turned into a bloodbath. Along similar lines, we expect that whoever replaces Sandra Day O'Connor—perhaps the swing justice to end all swing justices—will face a far bumpier road to confirmation than even Bush's candidate for the chief justice spot, who will likely be another conservative to replace a conservative. Timing may not be everything, as the saying goes, but it does count for something in the appointments game.

What also counts is the candidate's ideology, or more precisely the political compatibility (or lack thereof) between senators and the candidate. We, along with virtually all other observers of Supreme Court confirmations, suspect that senators are most likely to vote for nominees who are ideologically close to them (consider the conservative Republican senator Orrin Hatch and the conservative Republican nominee William H. Rehnquist) and least likely to vote for nominees who are ideologically distant from them (the liberal Ted Kennedy and Rehnquist), and this is exactly what we find.

To reach this conclusion, we examined the same 2,451 senators' votes we used earlier to analyze the effect of qualifications, only here we consider ideology. (See Figure 4.6.) To determine whether a nominee to the Supreme Court was liberal, conservative, or somewhere in between, we again relied on the assessment of newspaper editors—assessments that comport quite nicely with our overall impression of the nominees who ascended to the bench. (See Figure 4.7 for a description of our method.)[35] To be sure, there are some exceptions. For example, at the time of his nomination, the editors thought Clarence Thomas would be a moderate to conservative justice, but there is little about his voting on the Court that is moderate: he is a through-and-through conservative. But overall the fit between the scores and our impressions of those nominees who ascended to the Court is rather tight. William J. Brennan and Thurgood Marshall, liberal justices, were also assessed as liberals at the time of their nomination: both received the highest possible liberalism rating from the editors. So too, Antonin Scalia and William H. Rehnquist, regarded as conservative justices, were also regarded as right-of-center nominees.

A particular ideology, of course, can be a positive or a negative. For some senators, such as Orrin Hatch, Bork's conservatism made him a very desirable candidate; for others, such as Ted Kennedy, far less so. Accordingly, to examine the effect of ideology on confirmation votes, we compared the ideology of the nominee to the ideology of senators (using their

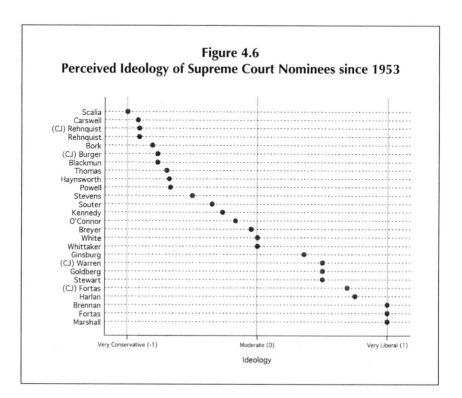

Figure 4.6
Perceived Ideology of Supreme Court Nominees since 1953

Figure 4.7
Assessing the Ideology of Supreme Court Nominees and Senators

Ideology of Nominees

We needed a measure that would work for all candidates to the Supreme Court (which eliminates votes or opinions, as not all Supreme Court nominees are judges) and which we could obtain prior to the Senate's vote. The method we use was developed by Jeffrey A. Segal and Albert D. Cover and relies on newspaper editorials written about the candidate between the time of his or her nomination to the Supreme Court and the Senate's vote. (Four newspapers were used, two liberal-leaning and two more conservative.)

The researchers read each paragraph in the editorial and determined whether the paragraph suggested that the nominee held moderate, conservative, or liberal views over particular issues. Liberal editorial statements include (but are not limited to) those suggesting that the candidate supports defendants in criminal cases, women and racial minorities in equality cases, and the individual against the government in privacy and First Amendment cases. Conservative statements are those in the opposite direction. Moderate statements include those that explicitly ascribe moderation to the nominees or those that ascribe both liberal and conservative values.

Segal and Cover then assessed the nominee's ideology by subtracting the fraction of paragraphs coded conservative from the fraction of paragraphs coded liberal and dividing by the total number of paragraphs coded liberal, conservative, and moderate. The resulting scale of ideology (or policy preferences) ranges from -1 (unanimously conservative) to 0 (moderate) to +1 (unanimously liberal), with Figure 4.6 displaying the score for each post-1953 nominee.

Ideology of Senators

Here we rely on the ideological scores assigned to each senator by Americans for Democratic Action (ADA), a liberal interest group. Each year, as the ADA explains it, its executive committee "selects 20 [congressional] votes it considers the most important during that session. Each member [of Congress] receives five points if he/she voted with ADA, and does not receive 5 points if he/she voted against us or was absent."

Based on these vote tallies, the most liberal senator could receive a total possible score of 100; the most conservative, 0. For example, in 1987, when President Reagan nominated Robert Bork, the liberal Democratic senators Ted Kennedy and John Kerry received ADA scores of 89 and 84, respectively. In contrast, the ADA assigned the conservative Republicans Jesse Helms and Orrin Hatch scores of 11 and 5, respectively. Al Gore, at the time a Democratic senator, fell somewhere between the two, with an ADA score of 58.

(continues)

Figure 4.7 (*continued*)

Comparing the Ideology of Nominees and Senators

To compare the ideologies of nominees and senators, we needed to convert the newspaper scores (which range from +1 to -1) and ADA scores (which range from 0 to 100) to the same metric. We added 1 to each editorial score and then divided by 2 (so Bork's -.81 becomes .095), and simply divided each ADA score by 100. Finally, we subtracted the senator's score from the nominee's and took the absolute value to remove negative signs. This provides us with a measure of the ideological distance between the two.

In other work, we have used different measures of senators' ideology (such as Keith Poole's NOMINATE scores, which are derived from analyses of votes cast by members of Congress) and different approaches to comparing senators' and nominees' ideology. All these methods produce similar results: Senators will most certainly vote for candidates who are ideologically close and well-qualified, and they also will almost certainly vote against candidates who are distant and not qualified.

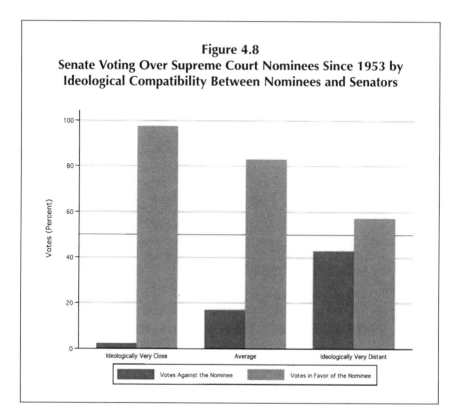

Figure 4.8
Senate Voting Over Supreme Court Nominees Since 1953 by Ideological Compatibility Between Nominees and Senators

voting records). Figure 4.8 displays the results of this comparison, and they are stark: nominees who are ideologically distant from senators receive only about 57 percent of their votes, but that figure jumps to 98 percent when they share a political outlook.

The Relationship Between Politics and Qualifications

Virtually from the day George W. Bush nominated Janice Brown to the all-important D.C. Circuit, controversy swirled around her. "Powerful liberal groups," to use Orrin Hatch's phrase, opposed her at least in part because, as a California Supreme Court justice, she had upheld restrictions on abortion rights and opposed affirmative action. Overall, they said, she was "even further to the right than the most far-right justices now sitting on the U.S. Supreme Court, Antonin Scalia and Clarence Thomas." Liberal interests, along with some senators, also asserted that she was unsuited for office. The National Organization for Women, for example, stated that "Brown was the first California Supreme Court Justice to receive an unqualified rating from the state bar and still be nominated by a governor. . . . Three-fourths of state bar evaluators felt Brown was ill-equipped to hold the position. Complaints filed by her peers called her 'insensitive to established legal precedent . . . and lack[ing] compassion and intellectual tolerance for opposing views.'"[36] And at the time of her nomination to the federal bench, the ABA evaluated Brown as "qualified," though a minority assigned her the lowest ranking, "not qualified."

The Senate eventually confirmed Brown by a 56–43 vote—but two years after Bush initially nominated her. She was the target of a Democratic filibuster that ended only after moderate members on both sides of the aisle drafted a compromise that enabled her confirmation.

Clearly, Brown's political values, not to mention her potential as a Supreme Court nominee, energized opposition from prominent liberal interest groups, which in turn lobbied senators to oppose her. But questions about her professional merit may have played a role too. In other words, all the factors we have considered—qualifications, partisanship, and ideology—probably contributed to the long delay and, ultimately, to the divided vote.

But was it merit or politics that exerted the greater influence? That is a hard question to answer for lower court nominees because the Browns are relatively few and far between.[37] The overwhelming majority of lower court nominations that reach the Senate's floor attain consensual confirmation.

But this is not true of candidates for the Supreme Court. Prior to the 1900s, the Senate rejected twenty of eighty-five candidates. And while senators' votes over most nominees since the mid-twentieth century have been unanimous or nearly so, of the 2,451 votes we examined, 378 were nays, or on average about 14.8 per nominee. Nor was dissensus wholly uncommon. In fifteen of the twenty-six cases the candidate caused some degree of division among the senators.

So what mattered more in these confirmation proceedings, ideology or qualifications? As our discussion thus far suggests, both exert a significant, independent effect on the Senate's decision to confirm or not. But it is the relationship between the two that provides the greatest explanatory power (see Figure 4.9). Senators will most certainly vote for candidates who are ideologically close and well qualified, and they also will almost certainly vote against candidates who are distant and not qualified. Moreover, the odds are high that they will vote for an undeserving candidate who is ideologically proximate (think of southern Democrats and Clement Haynsworth), thus underscoring the role of politics. But it is also the case that they will, under certain conditions, support a politically remote

Figure 4.9
Senate Voting Over Supreme Court Nominees Since 1953
(by perceived qualifications of the nominees and
ideological compatibility between nominees and senators)

Qualifications of the Nominee	Ideological Distance Between Nominee and Senator		
	Ideologically Very Close	Average	Ideologically Very Distant
Highly qualified	99.3	97.3	94.8
	(602)	(299)	(231)
Qualified	97.6	83.0	44.9
	(422)	(317)	(187)
Not qualified	91.8	38.5	1.7
	(182)	(96)	(115)

The upper figure in each box is the percentage of votes cast in favor of the nominee, based on all nominees in the category; the lower figure is the total number of votes in that category. So, for instance, of 602 votes cast by senators about nominees who were both highly qualified and ideologically close to the senator, 99.3 percent were cast in favor of the nominee.

candidate if they perceive that candidate to be highly meritorious (consider the example of Republicans and Ruth Bader Ginsburg), thus underscoring the role of qualifications.

So what went so right for Ruth Bader Ginsburg and so wrong for Robert H. Bork? Ginsburg is easy. Not only did newspaper editors on both the right and the left deem her meritorious, but so too did the ABA, which bestowed on her its highest rating, a unanimous "well qualified." On top of that, the Democratic nominee faced a friendly Senate, composed of fifty-six Democrats, along with a positive reception from the public. Polls taken at the time of her nomination reveal that Americans who had formed an opinion overwhelmingly supported her nomination, and their support only increased as the Senate vote drew closer.[38] Finally, ideology was not much of a factor. Despite her writings on the subject of women's rights and abortion, the press branded her only moderately to the left of center, or at least not much more liberal than the man she would replace, the Kennedy appointee Byron White. In short, based on our analysis, the chances of her *not* attaining confirmation were minuscule.

What of Bork? He himself blames interest groups and "the major media outlets," which he says were quite "hostile" to his candidacy. However, Bork fared better than he might suspect. He failed to receive a uniformly positive endorsement from the nation's press largely because of his role in firing the special prosecutor. But Bork's qualification rating was higher than Rehnquist's in 1986, a result of accusations that Rehnquist had harassed minority voters in the 1960s and lied about his role in a memo he wrote as a law clerk defending "separate but equal" schools in the *Brown* case. Likewise, he rated more highly than Stephen Breyer did in 1994, a result of Breyer's having voted in a pollution case that involved a company insured by Lloyd's of London, in which Breyer held stock.

To the extent that he was treated differently from other nominees, however, Bork is right. Prior to his nomination, large-scale opposition to Supreme Court nominees typically came only when the nominees were not well qualified, and then only from senators ideologically distant from the nominees. Republicans and southern Democrats jumped on Fortas's ethical lapses, while liberal Democrats jumped on Haynsworth's. To be sure, Bork faced questions about his role in Watergate. But his opponents did not use that as a justification for rejecting him; rather, opposition focused directly on his ideology. In this, Bork stands apart from the rejected nominees Fortas, Haynsworth, and Carswell and the near-reject Thomas. Because every nominee since Bork has been either ideologically moderate (Kennedy, Souter, Ginsburg, and Breyer) or perceived as unmeritorious (Thomas), it is too soon to tell whether this purely ideological opposition to an otherwise well-qualified nominee was an anomaly or a portent of changes to come.

What we do know, though, is that Robert Bork was not done in by his qualifications. Actually, had questions about his role in Watergate or about his professional merit been the only ones raised, our analysis suggests that Bork would now be a justice on the Supreme Court. It was the perception of his right-of-center ideology, or more precisely his ideological incompatibility with the Senate, that kept Bork from a seat on the high court.

5

Politics, Presidents, and Judging

Official photograph of Chief Justice William Rehnquist. *Richard Strauss, Collection of the Supreme Court of the United States*

Prior to 1984, the federal courts issued a number of "puzzling and relatively ad hoc" decisions over the question of whether they should defer to interpretations of federal law rendered by administrative agencies, such as the Environmental Protection Agency.[1] Sometimes courts respected the agency's ruling or even refused to examine it; other times they showed far less deference. This unpredictable state of the law changed markedly with the Supreme Court's decision in *Chevron v. Natural Resources Defense Council* (1984). In a now-landmark opinion, the justices declared that when a federal agency interprets an act of Congress, federal courts should defer to that interpretation so long as it is reasonable and does not violate the express commands of Congress.

Yet a funny thing happened on the way to implementing *Chevron*: Republican circuit court judges sitting on panels with two other Republicans frequently voted to reverse liberal agency decisions but were less likely to vote to overturn them if even a single Democrat served on the panel. Similarly, Democratic judges on panels with other Democrats frequently voted against conservative agency decisions but were less likely to reverse them if a Republican sat along with them. This pattern of behavior, some scholars argue, reflects the threat posed by a "whistleblower"—a judge on a circuit court panel whose political preferences differ from those of the other two members. Should the majority attempt to reach a decision that disregards the preferences of their judicial superiors, the justices of the U.S. Supreme Court, the whistleblower may be willing to expose the majority's deviant behavior by means of a dissent that might draw the attention of the high court and possibly lead to a reversal of the appellate court's decision.

To the federal appellate court judge Harry Edwards this argument is "absurd." "Appellate judging," to Judge Edwards, "is fundamentally a principled practice." Similarly, Judge Patricia Wald, writing about the same whistleblower theory, claims, "It would certainly be cause for acute concern that federal judges, constitutionally designed to be apolitical, appeared to be deciding cases based on political motivations. I do not think that is the reality, however."[2]

To the extent that Judges Edwards and Wald are correct—that judges and justices are truly principled decision makers—it should not matter much whom the president appoints to the bench, given a requisite modicum of legal training and intelligence. To be sure, differences in the interpretation of federal laws might result if, say, some judges give more weight to the plain meaning of legislation and others place more emphasis on its history, but overwhelming agreement ought still emerge over basic principles of law. On the other hand, if justices largely base decisions on their own political values, then, as Richard Nixon said, "the most important appointments a President makes are to the Supreme Court of the United States."[3] Circuit and district court judges may not be quite as important. But, as contemporary battles over nominees to these tribunals suggest, many presidents (and senators) assume that ideology fundamentally affects the decisions of lower court judges as well.

If this assumption holds, then it follows that presidents can influence the direction of legal policy by placing politically like-minded individuals on the bench—and, in some instances, influence it for many years to come. Franklin Roosevelt died in 1945, but two of his appointees, Hugo Black and William O. Douglas, stayed on the Supreme Court for nearly three more decades. Thirty years have elapsed since Jimmy Carter was elected president, but as of May 2005 eight of his appointees continue to serve as circuit judges. Thirty of the current 166 members of the federal appellate courts were seated by Ronald Reagan, and one Nixon appointee has remained on the Supreme Court into 2005 (William H. Rehnquist), while four continue to serve on the lower federal courts. Even more astonishing, a district court judge appointed by Lyndon Johnson in 1966, Manuel Real, has yet to retire.[4]

It is of course one thing for judges and justices to remain on the bench long after their appointing presidents have left office but quite another for those jurists to represent the interests of their president over the course of their (sometimes long) tenure. Do presidents succeed in appointing ideological soul mates to the federal bench? Are those appointees "political" or "principled" in their decision making once they become judges? And, perhaps most crucially of all, do their decisions, if they are in fact political, reflect the ideology of their appointing president? In other words, do presidents get what they want in the men and women they name to the federal judiciary, and if so, for how long do their legacies endure?

In what follows we explore these questions, focusing on presidential influence on the U.S. Supreme Court and the federal circuits. Throughout we provide a good deal of data to support our specific claims, but it is the larger point that should not be missed: at least in the short term and at least at the level of the Supreme Court, presidents are not wrong to think they can influence the law via their appointments. Federal judges, especially Supreme Court justices, are more often than not ideological rather than principled decision makers, and ideological in ways that their nominating presidents would applaud. This fact, as it turns out, brings us full circle in our quest to understand why the appointments process is and always has been mired in politics: it is at least in part because the outcomes of that process, federal judges and justices, are themselves political—and in rather predictable ways.

Do Presidents Get What They Want?
The Need for Systematic Evidence

Anecdotally, presidents are notorious whiners about their judicial appointees, especially to the U.S. Supreme Court. No discussion of presidential influence over federal justices is complete without Theodore Roosevelt's quip that he could "carve out of a banana a Judge with more backbone" than Oliver Wendell Holmes, or Truman's claim that Justice Tom Clark

(1949–1967) was "my biggest mistake." Eisenhower purportedly labeled his appointment of the liberal Earl Warren "the biggest damn fool mistake I ever made," and apparently thought much the same of the equally liberal William J. Brennan Jr. Likewise, we cannot imagine that Richard Nixon was pleased with the leftward turn of his once-conservative appointee Harry Blackmun, any more than George H. W. Bush probably appreciates the liberal trend of David Souter's (1990–) decisions.

According to the prominent Court historian Charles Warren, "nothing is more striking in the history of the Court than the manner in which the hopes of those who expected a judge to follow the political views of the President appointing him are disappointed." To Henry Abraham "there is a considerable element of unpredictability in the judicial appointing process." And to Chief Justice Rehnquist even policy-minded presidents will be only partially successful, in light of their inability to foresee what issues will come before the Court. Abraham Lincoln appointed justices who provided crucial votes on Civil War–related cases but deserted him on issues that arose after the war. Franklin Roosevelt seated justices who supported him on economic cases but split badly with one another over the civil liberties agenda that dominated the post–World War II era.

Famed constitutional scholar Laurence Tribe, on the other hand, refers to the "myth of the surprised president." By this he means that "in areas of particular and known concern to a President, Justices have been loyal to the ideals and perspectives of the men who have nominated them." Donald Lively agrees, using Rehnquist's own predictability as a staunch defender of law and order to deride the chief justice's claim that presidential attempts to pack the Court are doomed to fail.[5]

These anecdotes suggest nothing if not the need for more systematic evidence—and a chain of systematic evidence at that. Specifically, a demonstration of Tribe's basic contention that presidents get what they want in their justices (and judges) must show, first, that presidents appoint ideologically like-minded men and women to the bench and, second, that ideology affects the decisions of these nominees once they ascend to the bench. Finally, if presidents *do* get what they ask for, the demonstration must prove that the ideology reflected in the judges' decisions matches up with the ideology of their appointing president. Since it is not difficult to identify justices who were political in their decision making but departed from the ideology of their appointing president—indeed, Presidents Roosevelt, Truman, and Eisenhower, in pointing to their own "mistakes," have done it for us—this last step is especially crucial.

Presidents and Their Appointees

When the Republican Herbert Hoover chose Benjamin Cardozo to fill Oliver Wendell Holmes's seat on the Supreme Court, the president had no reason to believe that Cardozo shared his political values. Actually, quite the opposite: Cardozo was a Democrat and a progressive at that. Similarly, unless newspaper editors of the day knew something that Dwight Eisenhower did not, the president could hardly have believed that his nominee William J. Brennan Jr. would have emerged as even a centrist on the Court.

Motivating the president in both these instances were goals other than ideology: perhaps sheer merit in the case of Cardozo, and certainly electoral considerations in the case of the Democrat and Catholic Brennan. We would thus not necessarily expect these jurists to share their president's political outlook.

As it turns out, though, the Cardozos and Brennans are exceptions. The rule is that most presidents nominate political allies to the Court. To illustrate this we compared the ideology of presidents, based on their positions over bills before Congress,[6] and of their nominees, as assessed by newspaper editors between the time of nomination and Senate action over their appointment (see Figure 5.1).[7] If the ideology of the president corresponds to the ideology of his appointee(s), then we should see justices appointed by the conservative presidents Reagan, George H. W. Bush, Nixon, and Ford group toward the bottom of the figure. Similarly, justices appointed by the liberals Johnson, Kennedy, and Clinton should cluster nearer the top, and justices appointed by the relatively moderate Eisenhower should appear closer to the middle.

Overall, this is the pattern we observe: as presidents become more liberal, their nominees become more liberal as well. Ronald Reagan, the most conservative of the presidents we depict, appointed two of the most conservative justices, Rehnquist and Scalia. Lyndon Johnson, on the other hand, was quite liberal, as were his nominees, Abe Fortas (nominated twice, once for associate justice in 1965 and once for chief justice in 1968) and

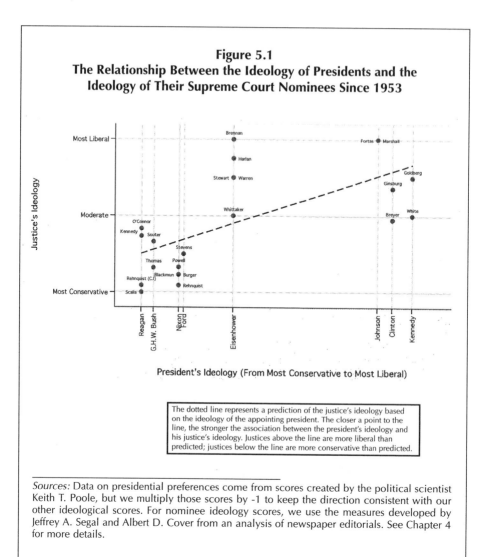

Figure 5.1
The Relationship Between the Ideology of Presidents and the Ideology of Their Supreme Court Nominees Since 1953

The dotted line represents a prediction of the justice's ideology based on the ideology of the appointing president. The closer a point to the line, the stronger the association between the president's ideology and his justice's ideology. Justices above the line are more liberal than predicted; justices below the line are more conservative than predicted.

Sources: Data on presidential preferences come from scores created by the political scientist Keith T. Poole, but we multiply those scores by -1 to keep the direction consistent with our other ideological scores. For nominee ideology scores, we use the measures developed by Jeffrey A. Segal and Albert D. Cover from an analysis of newspaper editorials. See Chapter 4 for more details.

Thurgood Marshall. Sitting toward the middle is Dwight Eisenhower, as is one of his nominees, Charles Whittaker (1957–1962).

Certainly, as we can also observe, the association between the president's ideology and his appointees is not perfect: the very liberal Brennan was out of political sync with the more moderate Eisenhower. Conversely, Byron White was somewhat to the ideological right of his appointing president, the liberal John F. Kennedy. But, looking across the spectrum, the Brennans and Whites emerge as the anomalies. Far more typical are the Rehnquists and the Marshalls—justices, whether on the left, on the right, or in the middle, who share the political preferences of their president.

That this rather strong association emerges between the presidents' and their justices' political ideology is not altogether surprising. Subject to the constraint of Senate confirmation, presidents are relatively free to name whomever they want to the Court, and their choice usually turns out to be an ideological ally.

But that does not always or even typically hold for appointments to the U.S. Courts of Appeals, for two reasons. First, presidents may be more likely to view these nominations as vehicles to advance their partisan or electoral ends rather than to attain policy goals. Whereas a judge chosen for partisan reasons, such as currying favor with an important senator, constituency, or interest group, might reap direct and immediate benefits for the president, electoral or otherwise, a judge selected to advance policy goals, in contrast, can have but a small influence on the ideological direction and impact of judicial policies. That is because decisions issued by appellate court judges have authoritative value only within the particular circuit and even there may not stand should the Supreme Court reverse them. For example, when a panel of Tenth Circuit judges (two of whom were appointed by Democratic presidents) upheld a federal program that provided incentives for contractors to employ minority-owned businesses, the decision came as welcome news to the Clinton administration, which had defended the program. But the president's victory was short-lived. A little over a year later, the Supreme Court vacated the Tenth's judgment and, in the process, made it far more difficult to sustain government programs that give preference to racial minorities.[8]

Second, even when presidents attempt to advance policy goals via appointments to the circuits, they may run into an obstacle well before the Supreme Court: senatorial courtesy. If senators of the president's party play a role in selecting (or blocking) appellate court judges, then the president's nominees are more likely to share the ideological commitments of their appointing senator rather than those of the president. An appellate court candidate proposed by the moderate Rhode Island Republican Lincoln Chafee, for example, probably would be left of center relative to a candidate that George W. Bush would name on his own.

Even so, it would be asking too much to believe that no relationship whatsoever exists between presidential ideology and nominees' political values. It seems inconceivable to think that Bill Clinton would have named the conservative Robert Bork to a circuit court but quite conceivable that Ronald Reagan would (and did). Likewise, Jimmy Carter's appointment of the moderately liberal Ruth Bader Ginsburg to the D.C. Court of Appeals seems entirely fitting with the president's own moderately liberal ideology. Had George W. Bush made that appointment, we would have been quite surprised.

Available evidence is consistent with these intuitions. As we reported back in Chapter 3, historically presidents have appointed members of their political party to the circuits, and George W. Bush is no exception: he has named but two Democrats to the thirty-four seats he has filled (through 2004).[9] Partisan attachment is hardly a perfect indicator of ideology, but it is not altogether uninformative. While the conservative senators Bill Frist and the moderate Lincoln Chafee are both Republicans, no one would mistake the conservatives Frist and Orrin Hatch for Democrats.

Likewise, while it is probably true that circuit nominees appointed under senatorial courtesy conditions are more likely to share the views of their appointing senator rather than the president's, it may be the case that senators and presidents from the same party are not altogether ideologically distinct. President Bill Clinton may have been slightly more liberal than Senator Herb Kohl (D-Wisc.), who was in the center of the ideological spectrum of Democrats for most of the Clinton years. George W. Bush is a bit more conservative than the median Republican in the Senate, currently Rick Santorum of Pennsylvania.[10] But in both cases the differences are relatively small, suggesting that while the president's courtesy appointments may be somewhat to the left (or right) of his political preferences, *somewhat* is the operative word. We simply would not expect vast discrepancies.

Appointees and Their Votes

The fit between the president's ideology and that of his nominees is interesting but for our purposes relevant only if nominees, once they become judges, vote on the basis of that ideology. To put it another way, if Judge Edwards is correct and jurists generally reach decisions based on shared legal principles or "neutral" values, rather than on their individual ideology, then it would matter not whether a president and his candidate held the same political values.

When it comes to the Supreme Court, even casual observers might dispute this idea of "neutral" judging. In December 2000, after the justices had cast the "votes that counted" in the presidential election, many Americans saw the *Bush v. Gore* decision for what it was: a thinly veiled attempt on the part of the Court's conservatives to put George W. Bush in the White House. Indeed, about 40 percent called it a "political" or "partisan" ruling.[11] The media also regularly describe justices in ideological terms, such as when they deem Antonin Scalia a "conservative," Sandra Day O'Connor a "centrist," and John Paul Stevens a "liberal."

These characterizations are not off the mark, as Figure 5.2 makes clear. To test the point, we examined the relationship between the justices' ideology and the votes they cast once seated on the Court. As before, we base our assessment of the justices' ideology on newspaper editorials written at

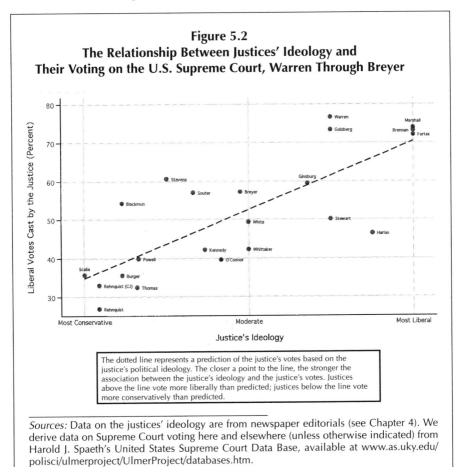

Figure 5.2
The Relationship Between Justices' Ideology and Their Voting on the U.S. Supreme Court, Warren Through Breyer

The dotted line represents a prediction of the justice's votes based on the justice's political ideology. The closer a point to the line, the stronger the association between the justice's ideology and the justice's votes. Justices above the line vote more liberally than predicted; justices below the line vote more conservatively than predicted.

Sources: Data on the justices' ideology are from newspaper editorials (see Chapter 4). We derive data on Supreme Court voting here and elsewhere (unless otherwise indicated) from Harold J. Spaeth's United States Supreme Court Data Base, available at www.as.uky.edu/polisci/ulmerproject/UlmerProject/databases.htm.

Figure 5.3
Assessing the Voting of Supreme Court Justices

Since the late 1980s, Professor Harold J. Spaeth has been collecting data on decisions of the U.S. Supreme Court and making those data available to the public. Among Spaeth's data is the "direction" of each decision, that is, whether the Court reached a liberal or conservative outcome. Spaeth's definition of these terms comports with conventional usage. "Liberal" decisions are those in favor of defendants in criminal cases; of women and minorities in civil rights cases; of individuals against the government in First Amendment, privacy, and due process cases; of unions over individuals and individuals over businesses in labor cases; and the government over businesses in economic regulation litigation. "Conservative" decisions are the reverse.

Spaeth also determines whether the vote cast by each justice was conservative or liberal. For example, he identifies *Roe v. Wade* (1973) as a liberal decision. So each of the seven justices who were in the majority of Roe were counted as voting in the liberal direction; the two who dissented were conservative voters.

To determine the liberal voting record of any given justice, we simply divided the number of liberal votes cast over the justice's career by the total number of votes cast. Since joining the Court in 1993, for example, Ruth Bader Ginsburg has voted in the liberal direction in 352 of the 516 cases that the Court heard and decided during her tenure (about 60 percent). Antonin Scalia, in contrast, cast only 593 liberal votes out of 1,746 (about 34 percent).

Source: Harold J. Spaeth's Supreme Court databases, along with the documentation necessary to use them, are available at www.as.uky.edu/polisci/ulmerproject/ UlmerProject/databases.htm. For more information about the data sets, see Harold J. Spaeth and Jeffrey A. Segal, "The U.S. Supreme Court Judicial Data Base: Providing New Insights into the Court," 83 *Judicature* 228 (2000).

the time of nomination. Justices are categorized as those with more conservative political values, such as Scalia, and those who are more liberal, such as Thurgood Marshall. (See Figure 5.3 for the methodology.) In Figure 5.2, justices who cast a high percentage of liberal votes are nearer the top (e.g., Earl Warren) than those who cast a low percentage (e.g., William H. Rehnquist).

If justices' votes reflect their political ideology, then the most conservative justices, such as Scalia, should be casting the lowest percentage of liberal votes. The most politically liberal justices, such as Brennan, should be casting the highest percentage of liberal votes. Moderate justices, such as Charles E. Whittaker, in contrast, ought to be near the center, casting neither many nor few liberal votes.

These are the very patterns we observe (see Figure 5.2). Indeed, with only scattered exceptions (e.g., the unexpectedly liberal voting of Harry Blackmun), the justices' ideology provides a remarkably good predictor of how they will vote on the Court. To take one example, Ruth Bader Ginsburg reaches liberal decisions in about 60 percent of the Court's cases—almost exactly the percentage we would expect from a justice with her rather liberal political outlook. Likewise, Antonin Scalia, assessed by virtually all evaluators as a conservative at the time of his nomination, votes precisely as that label would suggest, reaching right-of-center re-sults in almost seven out of every ten cases he decides. Seen in this way, Ginsburg's recent vote to uphold the University of Michigan law school's affirmative action program and her vote to strike down Texas's law pro-hibiting two persons of the same sex from engaging in sodomy were en-tirely as predictable as Scalia's vote to strike down the affirmative action plan but uphold the sodomy law.

Putting aside the protestations of those who continue to cling to the myth of neutral judging, we should not be too surprised by these results. While it is certainly true that many factors can limit the discretion of judges to reach decisions based on their policy preferences, they are not much in evidence for U.S. Supreme Court justices. These men and women have lifetime appointments and so no fear for their jobs. They also have a case-screening process that enables them to eliminate legally frivolous suits or those that virtually any judge would decide in the same way. There is no higher court above them, so they have no fear of being overruled. Finally, they have almost no ambition for higher office and, consequently, have little need to placate others. U.S. Supreme Court justices have more free-dom to act on their political preferences than those serving on any other court of which we are aware.

But, again, circuit court judges present a somewhat different picture: not only is the link between presidential ideology and nominees' ideology looser for the court of appeals, as we have already detailed, but so too is the link between judges' ideology and their votes.[12] To be sure, appeals court judges, like Supreme Court justices, have lifetime appointments, severely limiting the possibility of retribution for unpopular decisions.

House majority leader Tom DeLay (R-Tex.) can rail all he wants about out-of-touch, activist judges who refused to do the Republican party's bidding in the Terri Schiavo case (he declared that "the time will come for the men responsible for this to answer for their behavior," threatening impeachment by stating his desire to investigate precisely what constitutes the "good behavior" that guarantees their tenure), but nothing has come of this, and nothing will.

Even so, the appeals courts decide cases under circumstances different from those that apply in the Supreme Court. First, while the Supreme Court can weed out legally frivolous cases—those in which the law is so clear that no self-respecting judge could decide based solely on his or her policy preferences—the circuits have mandatory jurisdiction and must decide such cases. This means that many of their decisions are routine applications of existing law. Second, appeals court judges are limited by the fact that the Supreme Court can and does reverse their decisions. Reversals may be professionally embarrassing or perhaps even stand in the way of a promotion to the Supreme Court. Since most lower court judges hope to avoid reversals, judges may be unwilling to vote on the basis of their own political preferences if a potential whistleblower sits on their panel or if their own view of the legal question at issue is in conflict with the justices' clear-cut preferences. This is not to say, we hasten to note, that the circuits lack some discretion in deciding cases; rather, relative to the Supreme Court—indeed, because of the Supreme Court—that discretion is limited.

Data from any number of sources bear out both the political nature of circuit court voting and the limits of purely ideological voting. If we look strictly at the relationship between a judge's party affiliation—again, a rough indicator of ideology—and voting, patterns emerge over some legal questions but not others. Take the two politically charged areas of abortion and capital punishment. How does a judge appointed by a Democratic or Republican president vote when sitting on panels with all Republicans, all Democrats, or one Republican and one Democrat? In these controversial areas, the other members of the panel have virtually no effect on how judges vote. Democrats are far more likely to cast pro-choice votes (70 percent) than Republicans (49 percent), *period*. Likewise in capital punishment cases, Republicans vote in favor of defendants in 20 percent of the cases, in contrast to Democrats, who vote in favor of defendants 42 percent of the time.[13] For presidents seeking to place judges opposed to (or supportive of) the death penalty or abortion on the circuits, this is hardly a trivial finding: they can be reasonably confident that ideology (or, actually, partisanship) supplies some indication of how judges will vote.

On the other hand, abortion and capital punishment turn out to be rather odd areas—ones in which "antecedent convictions" are strong, or at least strong enough "to be relatively impervious to panel effects."[14] Other areas of the law, as we hinted at the beginning of the chapter, are not so impervious. In cases in which an industry challenges environmental regulations, Republican appointees tend to support industry and Democrats tend to uphold the regulations. But for these suits, unlike those involving capital punishment and abortion, the composition of the panel tends to amplify the ideological divide. When Republicans sit with all other Republicans, they support industry challenges to environmental regulations in about seven out of every ten cases. That figure, however, declines to five out of ten if even one Democratic whistleblower is on the panel. And should a judge find herself the lone Republican, odds are that she will rule *against* industry: in only four out of every ten cases do Republicans support challenges to environment regulations when they sit with two Democrats.[15]

This may be rather direct evidence of a whistleblower effect, and if so, it suggests that this effect is far more rampant than the sort of pure ideological (partisan) votes cast in capital punishment and abortion cases. Indeed, researchers have noticed panel effects in areas as disparate as affirmative action, corporate law, and campaign finance. In each, Democratic appointees tend to take more liberal positions and Republicans more conservative stances, but the composition of the panel can amplify or dampen those ideological tendencies.

Again, this is not to conclude that the ideology of a judge (in the form of the party affiliation of the appointing president) is irrelevant to his or her decisions. What with Democrats' appointees voting 74 percent in favor of affirmative action programs and their Republican counterparts voting in favor only 48 percent of the time, we cannot say that politics is irrelevant to circuit court judging—especially judging over politically salient issues. What we must conclude instead, and for all the reasons we noted above, is that circuit judges are not as free as Supreme Court justices to reach decisions that correspond to their sincerely held political values.

The President's Influence on the Courts

Having shown that presidents choose nominees, especially for the Supreme Court, with ideologies similar to theirs, and that the ideologies of the judges influence their voting behavior once on the bench, we must complete the picture by examining the relationship between presidential ideology and justices' voting behavior. This last step is necessary because even if presidents appoint ideological allies and even if those judges are ideological in their voting, it does not necessarily follow that the president gets what he wants. David H. Souter provides a case in point. When George H. W. Bush selected Souter to serve on the Supreme Court in 1990, the president had any number of reasons to believe that he was appointing a justice who would cast consistently conservative votes, whether over abortion, prayer in school, criminal rights, or affirmative action. Even newspaper editors (and editors of all ideological stripes, at that) agreed. Before Souter joined the Court, they deemed him to be relatively conservative, even more to the right than, say, the Reagan appointees, Anthony Kennedy and Sandra Day O'Connor, at the time of their nominations. As it turned out, Souter is a rather consistent liberal voter. These days he is far more likely to find himself voting with the liberal John Paul Stevens than with the conservative Antonin Scalia.

Our analysis of the justices' voting shows that Souter is not the only one to depart from the appointing president. When we compare the ideology of presidents with the votes cast by their justices, as we do in Figure 5.4, it becomes clear that Earl Warren is an even more dramatic case than David Souter. If Warren's voting corresponded with Eisenhower's political values, then we should observe Warren with few liberal votes. Indeed, based solely on Eisenhower's own ideology, we would predict a rather moderate Warren, voting in support of, say, criminal defendants as often as he voted against them. Another Eisenhower appointee, Potter Stewart, fits this description. But not Warren: he cast far more left-of-center votes (nearly eight out of every ten) than we would expect for an Eisenhower nominee.

Based on these data, it is no wonder that President Eisenhower deemed Warren a "mistake." Then again, if Eisenhower was paying off a campaign debt to Warren for delivering the California delegation during the 1952 Republican convention, as we explained in Chapter 3, then perhaps we should not be surprised by the lack of concordance between Eisen-

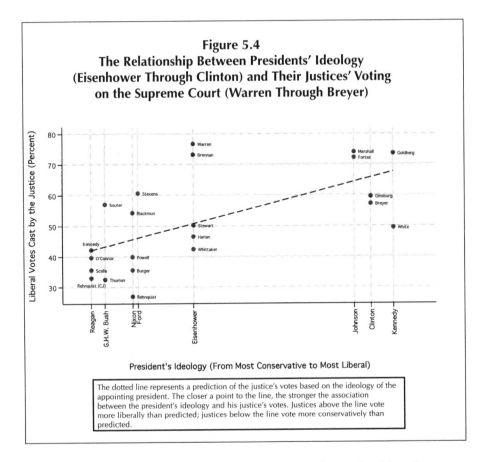

Figure 5.4
**The Relationship Between Presidents' Ideology
(Eisenhower Through Clinton) and Their Justices' Voting
on the Supreme Court (Warren Through Breyer)**

President's Ideology (From Most Conservative to Most Liberal)

The dotted line represents a prediction of the justice's votes based on the ideology of the appointing president. The closer a point to the line, the stronger the association between the president's ideology and his justice's votes. Justices above the line vote more liberally than predicted; justices below the line vote more conservatively than predicted.

hower's political views and Warren's votes. Nor, perhaps, should we be so surprised by Bush's Souter mistake—that is, another justice voting to the ideological left of his appointing president—though that may trace less to a campaign debt than to the Senate. While advisors (with the concurrence of newspaper editors) may have assured the president that Souter was a reliable conservative, Bush could have opted for any number of even more reliably solid conservatives; indeed, he seriously considered nominating Edith Jones, a very conservative circuit court judge. A problem for the Republican Bush was that Democrats dominated the Senate in 1991 and might not have confirmed a transparently reliable conservative candidate such as Jones. When confronted with Senates holding opposing political preferences, many presidents have compromised, making selections that come as close as possible to their own preferences without risking rejection in the Senate.[16] We have every reason to believe that after hearing that Jones would be a "strong 'in your face' political appointment," Bush followed suit with his selection of Souter. In this case, the divergence between his ideology and the justice's votes is understandable.

On the other hand—and this is the key point—"mistakes," regardless of why they occur, are few and far between. A visual inspection of the data in Figure 5.4 reveals that, by and large, presidents are successful with their appointees.[17] Most justices appointed by conservative presidents cast a high percentage of conservative votes. Ronald Reagan wanted conservatives when he appointed Kennedy, Scalia, O'Connor, and Rehnquist, and by and large got them. Likewise, most justices appointed by liberal presidents cast a higher percentage of left-of-center votes than their colleagues seated by more conservative presidents. So just as Reagan mostly succeeded in getting what he wanted from his appointees, so too did the relatively liberal Bill Clinton. Based solely on Clinton's ideology, we would expect both his justices, Ruth Bader Ginsburg and Stephen Breyer, to cast about 66 percent of their votes in favor of parties alleging a violation of their rights or against companies challenging environmental regulations. That prediction is not far off their mark: as we can see in the figure, Ginsburg and Breyer are, ideologically speaking, quite close, taking liberal stances in about 60 percent of the cases. Finally, while Eisenhower may have failed with Brennan and Warren—both of whom were considerably more liberal than the relatively moderate Eisenhower—he was far more successful with Potter Stewart, as we already pointed out, and also with his other two appointees, John Harlan and Charles Whittaker. The pair was slightly more conservative in their voting than we might have predicted based solely on Eisenhower's political values—but only slightly. Both cast about four out of every ten votes in favor of traditional liberal interests, rather than the five out of ten our analysis predicts.

Since most presidents have been sufficiently ideologically close to the confirming Senate to nominate nearly whomever they want, and many have actively sought to appoint justices who share their political outlook, Figure 5.4 is not particularly startling. But it is nonetheless suggestive. Politics pervades the appointments process, as we have stressed throughout, in part because the outcomes of that process—justices on the Supreme Court—are themselves political, and predictably so. More often than not, they vote in ways that would very much please the men who appointed them.

What of the circuit courts? Because the links between presidential ideology and judicial ideology and between judicial ideology and judicial voting are weaker, we expect a more tenuous relationship between presidential ideology and judicial behavior than we uncovered for the Supreme Court. This should be especially true for appointments made under the gun of senatorial courtesy, which may well produce judges more ideologically akin to home-state senators of the president's party (and perhaps to other state party leaders) than to the president himself.

Systematic data support these expectations. If we look only at the extent to which the typical (mean) circuit court judge took positions that were consistent with those of the appointing presidents in cases involving civil rights (e.g., race discrimination), civil liberties (e.g., free speech), and criminal justice (e.g., searches and seizures), then a stunningly close relationship emerges. The more liberal (or conservative) the president, the more liberal (or conservative) the votes of their appointees. So, for example, our analysis predicts, on average, that judges appointed by Reagan would cast only about 25.5 percent of their votes in favor of parties alleging a violation of their rights. The actual percentage is 25.7. Our predictions for liberal presidents, such as Lyndon Johnson, are equally on the mark. Based solely on Johnson's political values, we anticipate his appointees casting about 33.6 percent of their votes for liberal interests. Their actual support was 32.7—a rather trivial difference.[18]

We can imagine some taking these findings as proof positive that the myth of a "surprised president" is just that—a myth. Presidents know what they want in their lower court judges, and most of the time they get it. Jumping to that strong conclusion, however, would be a mistake. The problem is that the "typical" circuit court judge is not altogether typical. We make this point in Figure 5.5, which shows the voting patterns of individual circuit court judges appointed by Presidents Eisenhower through Carter.[19] While it is certainly the case that appointees of the most conservative president (Ronald Reagan) are, on average, more conservative than those named by Jimmy Carter (the most liberal of the eight presidents), some of Reagan's are actually *more liberal* than many of Carter's. Alternatively, Carter's most conservative appointee, the former law professor Jerre S. Williams, was nearly as conservative in his voting as Daniel A. Manion, a former Indiana state senator and the most conservative Reagan-appointed judge (both Williams and Manion cast fewer than two out of every ten votes in favor of parties alleging a violation of their rights). Likewise, while the liberal Carter did name the most liberal-voting judge in the sample (Stephen Reinhardt), Reagan did not appoint the most conservative one: William H. Timbers was seated on the Second Circuit by Richard Nixon. (Timbers, who died in 1994, had been an Eisenhower appointee on a U.S. District Court prior to his elevation to the Court of Appeals.)

In Figure 5.5 we looked at votes in cases involving rights, liberties, and justice, but the same basic patterns reappear in other types of litigation. Consider antitrust, an area in which President Reagan had relatively strong, anti-regulation (conservative) preferences, while Jimmy Carter was more favorably disposed toward regulation. Nonetheless, according to a study by William Kovacic, little difference emerges between the two sets of ap-

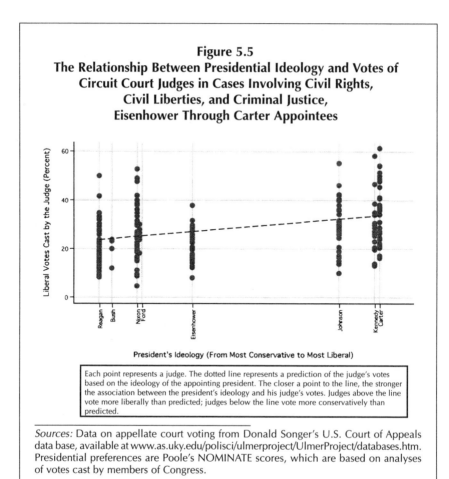

Figure 5.5
The Relationship Between Presidential Ideology and Votes of Circuit Court Judges in Cases Involving Civil Rights, Civil Liberties, and Criminal Justice, Eisenhower Through Carter Appointees

Each point represents a judge. The dotted line represents a prediction of the judge's votes based on the ideology of the appointing president. The closer a point to the line, the stronger the association between the president's ideology and his judge's votes. Judges above the line vote more liberally than predicted; judges below the line vote more conservatively than predicted.

Sources: Data on appellate court voting from Donald Songer's U.S. Court of Appeals data base, available at www.as.uky.edu/polisci/ulmerproject/UlmerProject/databases.htm. Presidential preferences are Poole's NOMINATE scores, which are based on analyses of votes cast by members of Congress.

pointees. Reagan's voted against regulation in just over 80 percent of the cases, Carter's in 70 percent. In fact, one Carter appointee, Stephen Breyer (now on the Supreme Court), *never* voted liberally in the antitrust cases studied by Kovacic, while one Reagan appointee, Richard Posner, who is the founder of the law and economics movement and who, to Kovacic, serves as "a meaningful benchmark of anti-trust conservatism," did so occasionally (20 percent of the time).[20] Overall, the results do show differences between Carter and Reagan judges, but they are not of the dramatic sort we routinely find among Supreme Court appointees.

On the other hand, the results (at least for cases involving rights, liberties, and justice) do become more (or less) dramatic if we take into account whether senatorial courtesy was in effect at the time of the nomination. When the president makes an appointment from a state in which one or both senators belong to the president's party—meaning that senatorial courtesy may be in effect—the relationship between presidential ideology and the judges' voting is not particularly strong. Actually, for these appointments, it is impossible to distinguish Lyndon Johnson's judges from Richard Nixon's! Alternatively, when a president makes an appointment without the constraint of senatorial courtesy—that is, when no home-state senator from the president's party participates in the nomination process—the resulting nominee is far more likely to share the president's ideology. For these appointments, the association between the president's political preferences and his judges' voting is quite respectable and, actually, not altogether different than the one we found for Supreme Court justices.[21]

Lasting Legacies?

That justices (and, under some circumstances, circuit court judges) vote in ways that reflect the political values of their appointing presidents is welcome news for those presidents, though it is probably no surprise. Less welcome is the conclusion that their influence may be more circumscribed than they may suspect or, of course, desire. Presidents may wish to sway individual jurists and the courts they serve, but the evidence that they do so is not as clear-cut.

Justices

While presidents can get what they want by appointing like-minded individuals to the bench, it turns out that time can dampen any legacy they hope to leave to the nation. For one thing, even if a president nominates an ideological ally, nothing prevents that ally from rethinking his or her jurisprudence over time. Witness Harry Blackmun, who early in his career on the Court joined the three other conservative Nixon appointees to uphold the death penalty. But just before he retired Blackmun declared that "no sentence of death may be constitutionally imposed" and that "from this day forward" he "no longer shall tinker with the machinery of death." Justice John Paul Stevens too has become increasingly liberal with each passing administration, while Byron White became increasingly conservative. As Richard Friedman notes, "No matter how important a Justice's substantive views may be, ideological consideration at the time of his nomination is futile to the extent that it is impossible to predict what those views will be over the course of his career on the Court."[22]

The passage of time also means that justices will be hearing issues to which their appointing president (and Senate) probably never gave much thought. While Abraham Lincoln's appointees supported him on cases related to the Civil War, they regularly rejected his views on crucial issues— military courts, legal tender, and the Fourteenth Amendment—that arose after the war ended (and after Lincoln was assassinated). Likewise, when Ronald Reagan appointed Anthony Kennedy, criminal law was a far more salient political matter to the president than, say, gay rights. Nonetheless, it was Kennedy who wrote the opinion disallowing states from prohibiting persons of the same sex from engaging in sodomy—an opinion that Reagan very likely would have condemned.

More systematic data confirm these anecdotes. During the first four years of justices' tenure, their voting behavior correlates at a rather high level (.64) with their appointing president's ideology, but for justices with ten or more years of service, that relationship drops to .49. In other words, liberal presidents appoint liberal justices who continue to take liberal positions *for a while*. Ditto for conservatives. But as new issues come to the Court, or as the justice for whatever reason makes adjustments in his or her political outlook, the president's influence wanes.

Sandra Day O'Connor, the Court's swing justice during her last few terms on the Court, provides a case in point. Over time, this Reagan appointee grew more liberal in her political preferences, as we show in Figure 5.6—and with that movement came a change in her voting behavior. So, for example, based on our calculations, the probability of the Court's upholding an affirmative action program just ten years ago was rather small

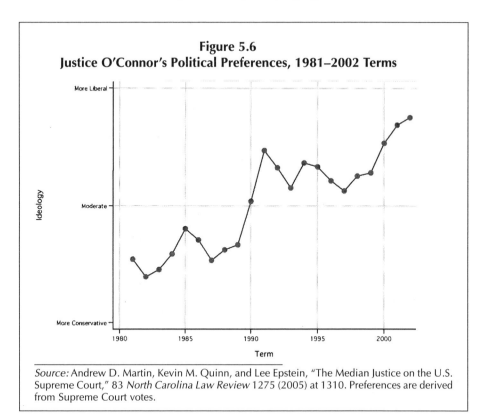

Figure 5.6
Justice O'Connor's Political Preferences, 1981–2002 Terms

Source: Andrew D. Martin, Kevin M. Quinn, and Lee Epstein, "The Median Justice on the U.S. Supreme Court," 83 *North Carolina Law Review* 1275 (2005) at 1310. Preferences are derived from Supreme Court votes.

(about .32); by the time the Court heard a challenge to the University of Michigan law school's affirmative action plan in its 2002 term, the odds had increased to over 50 percent—largely because of O'Connor's move to the left. At the end of the day, O'Connor did, in fact, provide the key vote to uphold the Michigan law program, surely a vote that her appointing president would have appreciated about as much as he would have liked Kennedy's opinion in the sodomy case.

Courts

Long-lasting legacies in the form of individual justices willing to maintain their appointing presidents' ideological commitments are possible but far from certain: much depends instead on the issues coming before the Court or on factors idiosyncratic to particular justices. Serendipity plays an even greater role in determining whether presidents can leave their imprint on the Supreme Court or entire circuits.

Take the case of Ronald Reagan. Few presidents had as much opportunity to influence the Supreme Court as he did. The conservative Republican reached out again and again to social conservatives, calling for the return of school prayer, the reversal of *Roe v. Wade* (1973), and reductions in the rights accorded to the criminally accused. While campaigning for Republican Senate candidates in 1986, Reagan argued that "the proliferation of drugs has been part of a crime epidemic that can be traced to, among other things, liberal judges who are unwilling to get tough with the criminal element in society. . . .We don't need a bunch of sociology majors on the bench."

Fate smiled upon the fortieth president, granting him four appointees to the high Court and the opportunity to fill hundreds of vacancies on the lower federal courts. Yet the Supreme Court he left was no more conservative than the one he inherited. Moreover, despite his appointees, the twentieth century ended with organized school prayer still unconstitutional and *Roe v. Wade* still the law of the land.

The more moderate Richard Nixon, in contrast, had a greater impact in pulling the Court to the right. The Warren Court, he declared in his 1968 campaign, had gone too far in protecting criminal forces in society. He wanted to replace liberals with justices who would not be, as we reported in Chapter 3, "favorably inclined toward claims of either criminal defendants or civil rights plaintiffs." Nixon won the election, earning the opportunity, like Reagan, to name four new members of the Supreme Court.

Though a variety of factors worked to constrain the conservative thrust of Nixon's Court—not the least of which was the president's own liberalism on issues such as the Equal Rights Amendment and affirmative action—Nixon was successful in ways that Reagan was not. Under the leadership of his chief justice, Warren Burger, the Court declined to declare capital punishment unconstitutional per se, and it limited the reach of the Warren Court's *Mapp* and *Miranda* decisions, which had restricted the use of evidence and confessions illegally obtained. The Burger Court increased the ability of states to ban obscene materials and refused to equalize state spending between school districts. It also turned down the opportunity to extend the right to privacy to homosexual conduct. In regard to colleges and universities that discriminate on the basis of sex, the Court ruled that they would lose funds for specific programs but not for the entire institution.

An analysis of the percentage of liberal votes on the Supreme Court during ten presidential administrations shores up the basic point of this story: presidents have had varying degrees of success in transforming the

Supreme Court. After the Eisenhower administration (in which 63.3 percent of the votes were liberal), the Court grew increasingly liberal during the presidencies of the Democrats John Kennedy (66.5 percent liberal votes) and Lyndon Johnson (68.0 percent), and then increasingly conservative when the Republicans Richard Nixon (50.3 percent) and Gerald Ford (44.4 percent) were in office—just as we might expect and just as those presidents would have likely desired. As the only modern-day president without the opportunity to appoint any justices, Jimmy Carter obviously had no impact on the Court. Yet Ronald Reagan, perhaps the most conservative president of the twentieth century, oversaw a Court that was only marginally less liberal (with 44.8 percent liberal votes) than it was during the Ford and Carter years, despite his four appointments to the bench.

Why some presidents seem to have more influence on the ideological direction of the Court than others has a good deal to do with the justices their appointees replace and not simply with whom the president nominates. At the time Richard Nixon took office in 1969, the Supreme Court consisted of Chief Justice Earl Warren and Associate Justices Hugo Black, John Harlan, William Brennan, Potter Stewart, Abe Fortas, Byron White, Thurgood Marshall, and William Douglas. On average, these justices were extremely liberal, voting about seven times out of ten in favor of parties alleging a violation of their rights or liberties. The four justices that Nixon replaced (Warren, Black, Fortas, and Harlan) were even slightly more liberal. The four he appointed, in contrast, were quite conservative, voting in favor of liberal interests in about a third of all cases, significantly lowering the Court's overall support for rights and liberties claims. On the other hand, while Ronald Reagan did place the extremely conservative Antonin Scalia on the Court, Scalia took the seat of associate justice William H. Rehnquist, another strong conservative. As a result, Scalia's appointment did not have a discernible effect on the direction of Court decisions. Nor did Reagan's other appointments. While they were conservative, they too supplanted other (relatively) conservative justices, leaving the president's short-run impact on the high Court fairly negligible.[23]

Similar problems afflict the president's ability to change the ideological direction of the courts of appeals. If, for reasons political or economic (see Chapter 2), few vacancies exist across or within the circuits, a president's influence will be negligible, obviously. But even when presidents are able to appoint many judges, moving the circuits is still no easy task.

Consider Bill Clinton. His appointments to the U.S. Courts of Appeals altered the ideological complexion of most; the Second and Sixth Circuits, in particular, moved considerably to the left (or at least to a position far more liberal than that of the Supreme Court) as a consequence of Clinton's judges.[24] But, in light of whistleblowers and other constraints on circuit judges, appointing more liberal judges does not ensure wholesale increases in liberal voting. Indeed, we already have shown that the relationship between the ideology of circuit court judges and their voting is generally weaker than it is for justices. This, in turn, suggests that presidents should have an even more difficult time shifting the ideological direction of the decisions reached by these courts than they do for the Supreme Court (which is no easy task either).

This is in fact the case. In direct contrast to the Supreme Court, almost no increase in liberalism occurs in the circuits during the Kennedy and Johnson administrations (22.7 and 21.2 percent liberal votes, respectively, compared to 20.1 percent during the Eisenhower administration). The highest levels of liberalism are during the Carter years (31.7 percent), but they are almost as high when Reagan was president (31.1 percent). Given that judicial appointments accumulate over the course of an administration, it is not surprising to see hints of a delayed effect. So, for example, the full impact of Johnson's appointees appears during the Nixon administration (when there were 28.0 percent liberal votes), while the full effect of the Reagan years appears during George H. W. Bush's administration (22.9 percent). Overall, though, shifting the direction of decisions produced by the courts of appeals proves much harder for presidents—and, despite recent political battles, of perhaps substantially less value—than moving the Supreme Court.

Packing the Courts

Given the discretion and power held by federal judges, especially Supreme Court justices, and the effect of their political outlooks in shaping how they use that discretion and power, Chief Justice Rehnquist finds it "normal and desirable for Presidents to attempt to pack" the judiciary:

> Surely we would not want it any other way. We want our federal courts, and particularly the Supreme Court, to be independent of public opinion when deciding the particular cases or controversies that come before them. The

provision for tenure during good behavior and the prohibition against diminu-
tion of compensation have proved more than adequate to secure that sort
of independence. The result is that judges are responsible to no electorate
or constituency. But the manifold provisions of the Constitution with which
judges must deal are by no means crystal clear in their import, and reasonable minds may differ as to which interpretation is proper. When a vacancy occurs on the Court, it is entirely appropriate that the vacancy be
filled by the President, responsible to a national constituency, as advised
by the Senate.[25]

Whether or not packing the courts is a laudable goal, a variety of factors can conspire against presidents seeking to achieve it. When it comes
to the lower courts, judges are constrained by the Supreme Court, and
presidents by the tradition of senatorial courtesy. Moreover, for judges
(and occasionally justices too), presidents may be more interested in pursuing
electoral or partisan objectives rather than those centering on policy. Such was
the case when Eisenhower selected the Catholic Democrat William Brennan
or when Reagan redeemed his campaign promise by naming a woman,
Sandra Day O'Connor, to the Court. So too, changing attitudes can rob a
president of the long-lasting influence he may have wished from one of
his justices.

But the public that elected Richard Nixon in 1968 desired and received
a more conservative Supreme Court. Though the Reagan revolution did
not make the courts substantially more conservative in their decision making, it did guarantee another generation of conservative domination, and
provided four of the five votes (all but that of Clarence Thomas, a George
H. W. Bush appointee) needed to select George W. Bush as the forty-third
president.

6

The Politics of Appointments Meets the Politics of Judging

Official photograph of Justice Sandra Day O'Connor. *George Augusta, Collection of the Supreme Court of the United States*

Fresh from his defeat in the Senate, Robert Bork declared that the political battle over his confirmation was a direct product of the "political decisions" made by the "modern" Supreme Court. "When the Court is perceived as a political rather than a legal institution," Bork declared, "nominees will be treated like political candidates."[1]

Bork is partially right. Judges are political, and their politics seeps into their decisions. But he is wrong to suggest that these are new phenomena. Judges and justices always have been political beings. Since the earliest days of the Republic, the vast majority of federal jurists have been affiliated with a partisan group and, in fact, have shared the party affiliation of the president who nominated them. On top of that, many, perhaps even a majority, attracted the attention of key players in the appointments process precisely because they had been active in party politics. Bork, the former U.S. solicitor general who fired the Watergate special prosecutor after two other members of the Nixon's Justice Department declined to do so, was hardly an exception; he was, in fact, closer to the rule.

Likewise, justices, and to a lesser extent judges, bring their politics into the courtroom—and always have. In the interest of dealing with the here and now, we have focused our analyses on judicial decisions since 1953 even though some of the justices serving during that period came to the Court much earlier (e.g., Justices Hugo L. Black in 1937 and William O. Douglas in 1939). Traces of political voting were not difficult to locate for this period, and they are not difficult to locate for earlier eras either. Chief Justice John Marshall was a proponent of a strong central government who tried to etch his philosophy into the law by enhancing the powers of the president, Congress, and, yes, the federal courts. Marshall's successor, Roger B. Taney, also held strong views about the role of the national government in society, but in the opposite direction: he wanted to minimize the central government in favor of states' rights. In the process, he precipitated the Civil War with his blatantly political decision in the *Dred Scott* case (1857). Moving into the twentieth century, the "Four Horsemen" (Justices Devanter, McReynolds, Sutherland, and Butler) were the bane of Franklin Roosevelt's existence, and their laissez-faire philosophy prompted FDR's court-packing plan. Finally, there is Robert Bork himself, a judge and Supreme Court nominee whose "neutral" approach to judging somehow led him to conservative answers on many legal questions. For each of these jurists, and others too numerous to list, it is clear that their political values infiltrated their decisions.

This is no slam on Robert Bork; actually, he and we fundamentally agree that the appointments process is political because federal judges and justices themselves are political. He also probably would agree with us that until judges and justices stop reaching political decisions, the process will never become any less political. Where we depart from Bork is in the possibility of this ever occurring. Bork says a return to neutral principles of law, such as allegiance to the intent of the framers, will depoliticize the process. We say there is nothing to return to. Political decision making and political decisions started in 1800, not in 1953 with the "modern" Court.

These days, some politicians and commentators have offered a different type of solution, suggesting that we eradicate life tenure for federal judges or even start impeaching them. This will not, of course, eliminate political judging; it will only make judges more politically subservient. A judge who holds views likely to get him or her in trouble with the existing regime (these days, an extremely liberal judge) will act in ways equally as ideological but in the reverse direction (these days, more conservatively).

Nor will this approach to the "problem" of political judging work to eliminate politics in the appointments process. As long as judges are political—

whether in ways that reflect their sincere political values or in ways echoing the government's—ideological and partisan considerations will infiltrate the process. And that is likely to be the case for a very long time.

If for this and no other reason, the current President Bush undoubtedly appreciates the importance of judicial appointments, especially to the Court that cast the decisive vote in the 2000 election. What is more, with O'Connor's departure and at least one more vacancy possible during his last term of office, and with a Senate (at least as it is currently constituted) sympathetic to his political outlook, this president may be well poised to leaving a lasting legacy to the nation. This legacy would come in the form of right-of-center jurists and, perhaps, a far more conservative Court. To be sure, a Rehnquist vacancy would have little punch. Much like the swap of Scalia for Rehnquist, Bush would simply replace a conservative with a conservative. But O'Connor's retirement opens up the possibility for substantial change in the direction of judicial policy, especially if the president manages to replace the swing O'Connor with another Scalia or Thomas, as he apparently desires. In the event that he succeeds, the resulting Court will likely take its place among the most conservative in contemporary (post-1930) American history—that is, until the next confirmation battle.

Notes

Introduction

1. We adopt and adapt the description of the Brandeis nomination from A. L. Todd, *Justice on Trial* (1964), Chapter 4, and Henry Abraham, *Justices and Presidents* (1999), at 136–137.
2. Five of the six Republicans voting against Bork (Weicker, Stafford, Chafee, Specter, and Packwood) were then among the ten most liberal members of their party. The remaining senator, Warner, is more accurately characterized as a moderate. We base these characterizations on Keith Poole's NOMI-NATE scores (available at http://voteview.com/dwnl.htm), which are derived from analyses of votes cast by members of Congress.
3. The quote from Socrates is in *Apology*.
4. The quote from C. Herman Pritchett appears in "Divisions of Opinion Among Justices of the U. S. Supreme Court, 1939–1941," 35 *American Political Science Review* 890 (1941), at 890.
5. The characterizations of the confirmation process as a "mess," "abysmal," "badly broken," and downright "disorderly, contentious, and unpredictable" are from, respectively, Stephen L. Carter, *The Confirmation Mess* (1994); Stephen Choi and Mitu Gulati, "A Tournament of Judges?" 92 *California Law Review* 299 (2004), at 301; Senator Dianne Feinstein, quoted in John Cornyn, "Our Broken Judicial Confirmation Process and the Need for Fili-buster Reform," 27 *Harvard Journal of Law and Public Policy* 181 (2003), at 184; Mark Silverstein, *Judicious Choices* (1994), at 6
6. Among the excellent books on appointments to the U.S. Supreme Court are Henry Abraham, *Justices and Presidents* (1999); David J. Danelski, *A*

Supreme Court Justice Is Appointed (1964); Richard Davis, *Electing Justice* (2005); John Massaro, *Supremely Political: The Role of Ideology and Presidential Management in Unsuccessful Supreme Court Nominees* (1990); Mark Silverstein, *Judicious Choices: The New Politics of Supreme Court Nominations* (1994); Laurence H. Tribe, *God Save This Honorable Court* (1985); David Alistair Yalof, *Pursuit of Justices: Presidential Politics and the Selection of Supreme Court Nominees* (1999). The best single book on nominations to the lower federal courts is Sheldon Goldman's *Picking Federal Judges* (1997). Also quite useful is Michael J. Gerhardt's *The Federal Appointments Process* (2003).We draw liberally from these and other volumes throughout ours.

Chapter 1

1. For centuries, judges in the United Kingdom held their positions at the pleasure of the king, and their terms of office expired on the death of the sovereign who had appointed them. This dependence on royal favor frequently made for judicial subservience. Their long struggle for free government convinced the English that an independent judiciary was vital to the type of constitutional rule they desired, but not until 1701 did the Act of Settlement provide that judges should serve during "good behavior"—meaning, short of some form of malfeasance, for life—with removal contingent upon parliamentary approval. And it was not until 1760 that judges' commissions did not expire on the death of the king who had appointed them. The newly established British practice of an independent judiciary was transplanted to America, where royal abuse of this principle was one of the grievances that gave a moral tinge to the Revolutionary cause. The Declaration of Independence accused King George III of having "made Judges (in the colonies) dependent on his Will alone, for the Tenure of their Offices, and the Amount and Payment of their Salaries."

2. For constitutional debates over the appointment of federal judges, see Max Farrand's authoritative *The Records of the Federal Convention of 1787* (1966), 4 vols. For a succinct summary (and excerpts) of the major controversies at the convention, see Daniel A. Farber and Suzanna Sherry, *A History of the American Constitution* (2005); Matthew D. Marcotte, "Advice and Consent: A Historical Argument for Substantive Senatorial Involvement in Nominations," 5 *NYU Journal on Legislation and Public Policy* 519 (2001/2002). Worth noting too is the extraordinary array of online documents about the Constitutional Convention housed at Yale Law School's Avalon project.

3. For an early analysis of rules governing the selection and retention of judges, see Evan Haynes, *The Selection and Tenure of Judges* (1944); for a more recent survey of practices in the United States and abroad, see Lee Epstein, Jack Knight, and Olga Shvetsova, "Comparing Judicial Selection Systems," 10 *William and Mary Bill of Rights Law Journal* 7 (2001).

4. According to the America Judicature Society, Massachusetts and New Hampshire provide life tenure until mandatory retirement. Rhode Island has full lifetime tenure.

5. Under the Judiciary Act of 1789 the Supreme Court was to have a chief justice and five associate justices. That the Court initially had only six mem-

bers illustrates an important point: Congress, not the Constitution or the Court itself, determines the number of justices. We return to this point in Chapter 2. Also worthy of note: while it is true that the Congress that passed the Act of 1789 was full of men committed to a strong central government, it would be a mistake to believe that the Act rejected all the claims of advocates of states' rights. To the contrary, in some important ways it contributed to the development of America's system of judicial federalism; for example, the Act used state lines as territorial boundaries for district and circuit courts. That Congress tied the boundaries to the states might have been a concession to states' rights supporters who wanted federal judges to have experience in the legal and political culture of a particular state. The practice of choosing district judges from the state and circuit judges from the region in which they will sit forms one of the bases of the rule of "senatorial courtesy," which, as we mention, gives a senator of the same political party as the president what amounts to almost a veto over important appointments in his or her state and further ties district judges and even circuit judges to localities. And senatorial courtesy is itself a by-product of federalism.

6. Administrative Office of the United States Courts, "Understanding the Federal Courts," provides an especially useful introduction to the federal judiciary (available at www.uscourts.gov/understand02/). We draw on this source and our own writings for Figures 1.2–1.5.

7. In *Katz,* Justice Potter Stewart wrote the opinion of the Court, but it is Justice John Harlan's concurrence that many commentators cite.

8. Chief Justice Chase's quote appears in *Ex parte Yerger* (1869). Note that not all nations have been willing to take that chance. Several European constitutions written in the twentieth century contain "McCardle clauses," which forbid the legislature to alter the jurisdiction of the highest court.

9. Though the judicial system in most states is three-tiered, eleven do not have intermediate appellate courts; litigants desiring to appeal their cases must go directly to their state's highest judicial body. In most of the remaining thirty-nine states, they have a right to appeal to an intermediate appellate court, just as they do in the federal ladder—meaning, in turn, that the bulk of state intermediate appellate work (as well as the work of the federal circuits) consists of hearing mandatory appeals from trial courts. Depending on the state, some types of trial court cases proceed directly to state courts of last resort; others must go first to intermediate appellate courts. In a handful of states, trial court cases are appealed directly to the state supreme court, which then decides whether an intermediate appellate court should hear the appeal.

10. Benjamin Franklin's quip appears in Max Farrand, *The Records of the Federal Convention of 1787* (1966), vol. 1, at 120.

11. For interesting articles on the intent of the framers over the judicial appointment process, see Henry Paul Monaghan, "The Confirmation Process: Law or Politics?" 101 *Harvard Law Review* 1202 (1988); David A. Strauss and Cass R. Sunstein, "The Senate, the Constitution, and the Confirmation Process," 101 *Yale Law Journal* 1491 (1992); John O. McGinnis, "The President,

the Senate, the Constitution, and the Confirmation Process: A Reply to Professors Strauss and Sunstein," 71 *Texas Law Review* 633 (1993).

12. The quote from John Adams appears in a letter to Roger Sherman, July 20, 1789, cited in John C. Eastman and Timothy Sandefur, "The Senate Is Supposed to Advise and Consent, Not Obstruct and Delay," 7 *Nexus Journal of Opinion* 11 (2002). The Nixon quote appears in the *New York Times*, April 2, 1970, at A28 and is cited in John Massaro, *Supremely Political* (1990), at 118.

13. The quote from Henry Abraham appears in his *Justices, Presidents and Senators* (1999), at 18.

14. The quote about "ideology—at least ideology . . . unrelated to a candidate's ability to fulfill his oath of office" comes from John C. Eastman and Timothy Sandefur, "The Senate Is Supposed to Advice and Consent, Not Obstruct and Delay," 7 *Nexus Journal of Opinion* 11 (2002).

15. Information on Supreme Court nominations appears in Lee Epstein et al., *The Supreme Court Compendium* (2003). Note that we, unlike others, do not count among the twenty-seven rejections George Washington's withdrawal of William Paterson. As Epstein et al. explain, Washington nominated Paterson on February 27, 1793, and withdrew the nomination the next day because of a constitutional technicality. Paterson had been a member of the U.S. Senate and had participated in the development of the Supreme Court in the Judiciary Act of 1789. Article I, Section 6 of the Constitution stipulates that no member of Congress "during the time for which he was elected" can be appointed to any office created during his term. Although Paterson was no longer a senator (he resigned in 1790 to become governor of New Jersey), the Senate term to which he was originally elected would not expire until March 4, 1793. Washington waited four more days and resubmitted the nomination. Paterson was confirmed the same day. The data on rejections to the district and court of appeals come from Denis Steven Rutkus and Mitchel A. Sollenberger, "Judicial Nomination Statistics: U.S. District and Circuit Courts, 1977–2003," Congressional Research Service, RL31635, February 23, 2004, Table 2(b). For the G. W. Bush administration we used the following figures: 35 confirmations out of 51 nominees to the courts of appeals, and 162 confirmations out of 174 nominees to the district courts.

16. Senator Robert P. Griffin was the one who said that senators actually nominate lower court judges. He made the comment in 1969 and it is cited in Betsy Palmer, "Evolution of the Senate's Role in the Nomination and Confirmation Process," Congressional Research Service, RL31948, June 5, 2003.

17. If there is no senator for that state from the president's party, the president will consult with party leaders or other political figures from that state.

18. We thank Sarah Binder of George Washington University and the Brookings Institution for supplying us with information on the Senate's use of filibusters.

19. The quote from Patrick Leahy appears in the *Congressional Record*, March 7, 2000.

20. Data on the party affiliation of lower court appointees are from Deborah J. Barrow, Gary Zuk, and Gerard S. Gryski, *The Federal Judiciary and Institutional Change* (1996) (Grant through G. H. W. Bush); Sheldon Goldman et al., "W. Bush Remaking the Judiciary: Like Father Like Son," 86 *Judicature* 282 (2003) (Clinton); Sheldon Goldman et al., "W. Bush's Judiciary: The First Term Record," 88 *Judicature* 244 (2005) (G. W. Bush, first term). Data on the party affiliation of Supreme Court nominees are from Lee Epstein, Jeffrey A. Segal, Harold J. Spaeth, and Thomas G. Walker, *The Supreme Court Compendium* (2003). We begin with Grant in 1869, as did Barrow and her colleagues, because of the relatively small number of positions on the federal bench prior to that time. So, for example, between 1789 and 1868, presidents filled a total of 192 seats; over the course of the next six decades (1869–1932) that figure was over three times as large (595). See Barrow et al., *The Federal Judiciary and Institutional Change,* at 28 (Table 3.1).

Chapter 2

1. Our discussion of the Fortas appointment draws from Henry Abraham, *Justices, Presidents, and Senators* (1999), at 212–217; David L. Stebenne, *Arthur J. Goldberg: New Deal Liberal* (1996), at 348–351; and the accessible, succinct biography based on Stebenne's work, available at http://goldberg.law.northwestern.edu/mainpages/bio.htm.

2. The Henry Hyde quote appears in *Congressional Record,* volume 124, part 2, at 2451. Earlier in the debate, Robert McClory (R-Ill.) also commented on the large number of judgeships being created: "It should not be overlooked that the large number of judgeships authorized by the bill has been made necessary by political maneuvering in prior Congresses. In 1976, the committee reported to the House a district judgeship bill containing 49 judgeships. Although that bill was amended by me to delay the effective date until a newly elected administration was sworn in and thus keep the bill out of politics, some House Members were fearful that President Ford would be reelected, and the bill was killed. Just 14 months later the committee voted to recommend 110 judgeships—more than double the previous number." *Congressional Record,* volume 124, part 2, at 2445.

3. For an analysis of Jefferson's "impeachment strategy," see Jack Knight and Lee Epstein, "On the Struggle for Judiciary Supremacy," 30 *Law and Society Review* 87 (1996).

4. The thirteen cases were as follows (in each instance the House voted to impeach, and it was up to the Senate to acquit or convict; the outcome is given in parentheses): 1804, John Pickering, district court, charged with making decisions contrary to law, failure to hear witnesses or allow an appeal contrary to law, and intoxication while on the bench (convicted); 1805, Samuel Chase, Supreme Court, charged with "arbitrary . . . and oppressive behavior" in conducting trials and subjecting a grand jury to a "political harangue" (acquitted); 1831, James Peck, district court, charged with abuse of contempt power (acquitted); 1862, West Humphreys, district court, charged

with supporting the Confederacy and failing to hold court (convicted); 1873, Mark H. Delhay, district court, charged with "intoxication off the bench as well as on the bench" (judge resigned after he was impeached but before the Senate's trial); 1905, Charles Swayne, district court, charged with failure to live in district as required by law, use of private railroad car, overstating expenses, and abusing contempt power (acquitted); 1912, Robert Archibald, commerce court, charged with improperly using his influence to enter into business dealings with potential litigants and improper appointment of a jury commissioner (convicted); 1926, George W. English, district court, charged with abuse of power, favoritism, and tyrannical and oppressive behavior (judge resigned after he was impeached but before the Senate's trial); 1933, Harold Louderback, district court, charged with favoritism and official financial improprieties (acquitted); 1936, Halsted L. Ritter, district court, charged with favoritism in appointments of receivers, practicing law, and bringing disrepute on the federal judiciary (convicted); 1986, Harry E. Claiborne, district court, charged with bringing his court into scandal and disrepute for having been sentenced to two years in jail for filing false tax returns (convicted); 1989, Alcee L. Hastings, district court, charged with conspiring to solicit a bribe, fabricating evidence in his criminal trial, leaking confidential information, and bringing disrepute on the federal courts (convicted); 1989, Walter L. Nixon, district court, charged with perjury before a federal grand jury and bringing disrepute on the federal courts (convicted). Data on impeachments here and in the main text are from Emily Van Tassel and Paul Finkelman, *Impeachable Offenses* (1999). See also Van Tassel's interesting article, "Resignations and Removals: A History of Federal Judicial Service—and Disservice—1789–1992," 142 *University of Pennsylvania Law Review* 333 (1993).

5. McCloskey made this statement in 1970 during House debate on the impeachment of William O. Douglas. An excerpt appears in Emily Van Tassel and Paul Finkelman, *Impeachable Offenses* (1999), at 61–67.

6. The figure of 1,271 departures between 1945 and 2000 comes from Albert Yoon, "Love's Labor Lost? Judicial Tenure Among Federal Court Judges: 1945–2000," 91 *California Law Review* 1029 (2003). Actually, when eligible judges are contemplating leaving the federal bench, they can permanently retire or take "senior status." If they choose the latter—a position created by Congress in 1919—they continue to hear cases, though on a reduced basis. Moreover, even though senior judges relinquish their seats and receive the same level of pension as those permanently retiring, they are entitled to any subsequent pay raises authorized by Congress. For more information, see Albert Yoon, "As You Like It: Senior Federal Judges and the Political Economy of Judicial Tenure," 2 *Journal of Empirical Legal Studies* (2005), forthcoming. The figure of 572 new judgeships between 1945 and 2000 includes the U.S. Court of Appeals for the Federal Circuit; excluding that court lowers the number to 560. These data are available at the Federal Judicial Center's Web site (www.fjc.gov/public/home.nsf/his).

7. Rehnquist's comments about judicial salary are from William H. Rehnquist, appearing before the National Commission on the Public Service. Reported in 34 *The Third Branch* 1 (2002). Available at www.uscourts.gov/ttb/july02ttb/july02.html.

8. Information about Robert Grier and the 1869 pension law draws on Charles Fairman's classic, "The Retirement of Federal Judges," 51 *Harvard Law Review* 397 (1938) and David J. Garrow's fascinating study, "Mental Decrepitude on the U.S. Supreme Court: The Historical Case for a 28th Amendment," 67 *University of Chicago Law Review* 995 (2000). We also draw on Garrow for our discussion of Sherman Minton. For another interesting account, see Alpheus Thomas Mason, "Politics and the Supreme Court: President Roosevelt's Proposal," 85 *University of Pennsylvania Law Review* 659 (1937).

9. Our discussion of the history of pension laws draws on Albert Yoon's wonderful paper, "The End of the Rainbow: Understanding Turnover Among Federal Judges," 7 *American Law and Economics Review* (2005), forthcoming. The data we cite on retirements come from this paper.

10. The quote from Minton appears in David J. Garrow, "Mental Decrepitude on the U.S. Supreme Court: The Historical Case for a 28th Amendment," 67 *University of Chicago Law Review* 995 (2000), at 1043.

11. The papers we cite on the politics of judicial retirements from appellate courts are David C. Nixon and J. David Haskin, "Judicial Retirement Strategies," 28 *American Politics Quarterly* 458 (2000), and James F. Spriggs II and Paul J. Wahlbeck, "Calling It Quits: Strategic Retirement on the Federal Courts of Appeals, 1893–1991," 48 *Political Research Quarterly* 573 (1995). See also Deborah J. Barrow and Gary Zuk, "An Institutional Analysis of Turnover in the Lower Federal Courts, 1900–1987," 52 *Journal of Politics* 457 (1990).

12. O'Connor's remark was first reported in Evan Thomas and Michael Isikoff, "The Truth Behind the Pillars," *Newsweek,* December 25, 2000, at 46, and was subsequently reported in numerous other publications.

13. Rehnquist's comment on retirements comes from an interview with Charlie Rose (PBS television broadcast, January 13, 1999), quoted in Artemus Ward, *Deciding to Leave: The Politics of Retirement from the United States Supreme Court* (2003), 218.

14. Throughout the section on the creation of new appellate court seats, we make use of John M. de Figueiredo and Emerson H. Tiller's "Congressional Control of the Courts: A Theoretical and Empirical Analysis of Expansion of the Federal Judiciary," 39 *Journal of Law and Economics* 435 (1996). The idea that "waiting for a sitting judge to die or retire is hardly the most efficient way for political actors to gain control of the U.S. judiciary" also comes from this paper. See also Deborah J. Barrow, Gary Zuk, and Gerard S. Gryski, *The Federal Judiciary and Institutional Change* (1996).

15. Information on the 1801 Judiciary Act comes from George I. Haskins and Herbert A. Johnson, *History of the Supreme Court of the United States,* Volume II: *Foundations of Power: John Marshall, 1801–1815* (1981); for

the events leading up to passage of the 1891 Act, see Felix Frankfurter and James M. Landis, *The Business of the Supreme Court* (1928).

16. Information on the number of authorized U.S. judgeships is available from the Federal Judicial Center at www.fjc.gov/public/home.nsf/hisc. Here we exclude specialized courts, such as the Court of International Trade, but include the U.S. Court of Appeals for the Federal Circuit, which was established in 1982 and houses twelve judges. We also exclude temporary judgeships that Congress never made permanent.

17. Data on the effect of litigation on bench expansions are from John M. de Figueiredo and Emerson H. Tiller's "Congressional Control of the Courts: A Theoretical and Empirical Analysis of Expansion of the Federal Judiciary," 39 *Journal of Law and Economics* 435 (1996), which we supplemented with data derived from the Federal Judicial Center's Web site, www.fjc.gov/public/home.nsf/hisc. Our discussion of the impact on judicial workload on bench expansion pertains only to the circuits. When it comes to the U.S. district courts, we might expect legislators to be more receptive to complaints of inefficiencies and injustice from their constituents, since these courts are more "local" in character than the circuits—recall, each state has at least one district court, whereas they share appellate courts—and that is in fact the case. When workloads have skyrocketed, as they have in contemporary times, Congress tends to expand the federal trial court bench. We draw this point from John M. de Figueiredo, Gerard Gryski, Emerson Tiller, and Gary Zuk, "Congress and the Political Expansion of the U.S. District Courts," 2 *American Law and Economics Review* 107 (2000). On the other hand, we should not discount the role of politics. Since 1789, there have been 136 expansions of the nation's trial courts, with fully 111 (or 81.6 percent) coming in periods of unified government. Data obtained from the Federal Judicial Center's Web site, www.fjc.gov/public/home.nsf/hisc.

18. The full quotes from Republicans supporting a split of the Ninth Circuit are from John Ensign of Nevada ("My proposal for division of the Ninth Circuit . . . provides for judicial expediency well into the future. By creating a new Twelfth and Thirteenth Circuit, we are able to grapple with the booming populations of the Sunbelt states and provide better administration to the people of the new Ninth Circuit") and Jeff Sessions ("We share a concern . . . about the terrible backlog of appeals that have built up in the Ninth Circuit").

19. By our calculations, a litigant in the Ninth has a one in four chance of having her case heard by three judges appointed by Democratic presidents; those odds fall to one in five in the Second, the next most Democratic circuit, and to near zero in the First, Fourth, Fifth, Seventh, and Eighth.

20. Some Democrats who oppose splitting the Ninth have done so on "principled" grounds, claiming that it is a costly (as much as $120 million), unnecessary endeavor. But other Democratic legislators have been quite forthright about the role of politics: "Now before the Senate are two different proposals to split the Ninth Circuit. . . . I have long regarded political attempts to alter the makeup and structure of our federal judiciary with some

skepticism. I do not support politicizing the bench with ideological appointments and I do not support politicizing the bench with geographical alterations to suit the current political winds," said the Democratic senator Patrick Leahy. The chief judge of the Ninth (and a Jimmy Carter appointee), Mary M. Schroeder, apparently agrees. When asked about her take on proposals to split the Ninth, she replied, "The driving force . . . is the desire of some political interests to want to have a court that can be controlled by those political interests. I think that behind it all is pretty much politics."

21. The quote from President Roosevelt comes from his White House radio broadcast, March 9, 1937. In the text we say that Franklin Roosevelt predicated his court-packing plan of 1937 at least in part on the argument that the judiciary was too overworked and understaffed to carry out its duties effectively. The other part was politics; indeed, the president was quite clear that his plan also was designed "to bring to the decision of social and economic problems younger men who have personal experience and contact with modern facts and circumstances under which average men have to live and work. This plan will save our national Constitution from hardening of the judicial arteries." This was an indirect dig at the ideological direction of decisions produced by the federal judiciary. He took a more direct swipe at the Supreme Court, saying that it "has improperly set itself up as a third House of the Congress—a super-legislature . . . reading into the Constitution words and implications which are not there, and were never intended to be there."

22. Data on public support for FDR's court-packing plan are available in Lee Epstein et al., *The Supreme Court Compendium* (2003), Table 8-28. The last polls taken (June 9–June 14) show a bit of an upswing in support for the plan but overall support declined over time.

23. There is no shortage of scholarly and popular treatments of the court-packing plan. Our discussion draws on Lee Epstein and Thomas G. Walker, *Constitutional Law for a Changing America: Institutional Powers and Constraints* (2004), which in turn relies on research by Gregory A. Caldeira, "Public Opinion and the U.S. Supreme Court: FDR's Court-Packing Plan," 81 *American Political Science Review* 1139 (1987); William E. Leuchtenburg, *Franklin Roosevelt and the New Deal, 1932–1940* (1963) and his "FDR's Court Packing Plan: A Second Life, a Second Death," *Duke Law Journal* 673 (1985).

Chapter 3

1. The quote about Fortas being "the best lawyer in America" is from Mark Silverstein, *Judicious Choices* (1994), at 10.

2. For more on the Sandra Day O'Connor nomination, see David Alistair Yalof, *Pursuit of Justices* (1999).

3. We draw on the work of Sheldon Goldman, who has written extensively on the personal, partisan, and policy goals of presidents. See his *Picking Federal Judges* (1997).

4. Several studies examine the extent to which courts, judges, and other law-related matters figure into elections. Among the most recent is William G. Ross, "The Role of Judicial Issues in a Presidential Campaign," 42 *Santa Clara Law Review* 391 (2002).

5. The quote from Bush is from the first presidential debate, October 3, 2000 (CNN transcript).

6. The quote from Bruce Ackerman appears in "The Court Packs Itself," in the *American Prospect*, February 12, 2001 (online version).

7. Data are from the Federal Judicial Center's Biographical Database, at www.fjc.gov/public/home.nsf/hisj.

8. We draw information on Clinton's involvement in judicial selection from David Alistair Yalof, *Pursuit of Justices* (1999), and Sarah Wilson, "Appellate Judicial Appointments During the Clinton Presidency: An Inside Perspective," 5 *Journal of Appellate Practice and Process* 29 (2003).

9. For data on nominations to the federal courts made by presidents since Truman, see Mitchel A. Sollenberger, "Judicial Nomination Statistics: U.S. District and Circuit Courts, 1945–1976." Congressional Research Service, RL32122, October 22, 2003; Denis Steven Rutkus and Mitchel A. Sollenberger, "Judicial Nomination Statistics: U.S. District and Circuit Courts, 1977–2003," Congressional Research Service, RL31635, February 23, 2004.

10. Information about the Federalist Society is available at its Web site; www.fed-soc.org/. Data on its influence over Bush's nominations are from "Blocking Judicial Ideologues," *New York Times*, April 27, 2001, at 24A.

11. The story about Franklin Pierce's appointment of John Campbell appears in Henry J. Abraham, *Justice, Presidents, and Senators* (1999), at 84. Dean's account of Burger's participation is in John W. Dean, *The Rehnquist Choice* (2001), at 137–138. Nixon, incidentally, may have nominated Lillie, but his attitude was revealed when Mitchell told the president, "It's going to be a very grave shock to [Burger]," to which Nixon replied: "It's a shock to me, for Christ sakes! I don't even think women should be educated."

12. The poll on Rehnquist was conducted by the Associated Press, on November 21, 2004. The question was "Please tell me, if you know, what job or political office is now held by William Rehnquist," and 19 percent said chief justice, 19 percent said a Supreme Court justice, and 62 percent weren't sure or gave another answer. The poll on Supreme Court justices more generally was taken by Fox News on July 1, 2003. The question was "Which one of the current Supreme Court Justices do you most admire or agree with?" and O'Connor was the only one to elicit a double-digit response (11 percent); 68 percent said they did not know any names. The Helms quote appears in Deborah Sontag, "The Power of the Fourth," *New York Times*, March 9, 2003, Sec. 6, at 40.

13. L. Marvin Overby et al. discuss the connection between a senator's black constituency and his or her voting over Thomas in "Courting Constituents? An Analysis of the Senate Confirmation Vote on Justice Clarence Thomas,"

86 *American Political Science Review* 997 (1992). Data on Arlen Specter are from CQ's Voting and Elections Collections, available at http://library.cqpress.com/elections. Robin M. Wolpert and James G. Gimpel, "Information, Recall, and Accountability: The Electorate's Response to the Clarence Thomas Nomination," 22 *Legislative Studies Quarterly* 535 (1997), provide data on the effect of the Thomas nomination on the 1992 elections.

14. The story about the Senate Foreign Relations Committee appears in Sheldon Goldman, *Picking Federal Judges* (1997), at 41.

15. The quote from George Washington is in John C. Patrick, ed. *The Writings of George Washington* (1940), vol. 34, at 488. Quoted in William J. Daniels, "The Geographic Factor in Appointments to the United States Supreme Court: 1789–1976," 31 *Western Political Quarterly* 226 (1978). The data in the paragraph also come from Daniels's article.

16. For Carter's commitment to human rights in terms of his judicial appointments, see Mary L. Clark, "Carter's Groundbreaking Appointment of Women to the Federal Bench: His Other 'Human Rights' Record," 11 *American University Journal of Gender, Social Policy and Law* 1131 (2003).

17. For an examination of the importance of symbolic politics, see Stephen P. Nicholson, Adrian D. Pantoja, and Gary Segura, "Ich bin ein Latino," available on Segura's Web site, www.uiowa.edu/~c030319.

18. Data on Hispanic appointees are from Sheldon Goldman et al., "W. Bush's Judiciary: The First Term Record," 88 *Judicature* 244 (2005).

19. The Rehnquist memorandum appears in John W. Dean, *The Rehnquist Choice* (2001), at 16.

20. The quote from G. W. Bush is from the first presidential debate, October 3, 2000 (CNN transcript).

21. Data on partisanship are from Sheldon Goldman et al., "W. Bush's Judiciary: The First Term Record," 88 *Judicature* 244 (2005).

22. Overall, more than 50 percent of those appointed to the federal courts since Franklin Roosevelt's time have been party activists, with most presidents appointing over 60 percent activists. Invariably, the courts of appeals appointees include more activists than those appointed to the district courts. Data are from Sheldon Goldman et al., "W. Bush's Judiciary: The First Term Record," 88 *Judicature* 244 (2005) and Sheldon Goldman, *Picking Federal Judges* (1997).

23. The story about Grant is from Henry J. Abraham, *Justice, Presidents, and Senators* (1999), at 95.

24. See Sheldon Goldman et al., "W. Bush's Judiciary: The First Term Record," 88 *Judicature* 244 (2005).

25. We draw on David Alistair Yalof, *Pursuit of Justices* (1999), at 354, for information on the Anthony Kennedy nomination.

26. The account about Roosevelt and the New Hampshire Justice appears in Sheldon Goldman, *Picking Federal Judges* (1997), at 33, 37–38.

27. For more on the battle cry "No more Souters," see Neil A. Lewis, "Mixed Results for Bush in Battles over Judges," *New York Times*, October 22, 2004,

at 1A; on conservatives' displeasure with Justice Anthony Kennedy, see Jason DeParle, "In Battle to Pick Next Justice, Right Says Avoid a Kennedy," *New York Times,* June 27, 2005, at 1A.

28. The account of Bork as an "ideal justice" draws on David Alistair Yalof, *Pursuit of Justices* (1999), at 147.

29. Financial reports and questionnaires of Bush nominees (mostly those filled out for the Senate) are available at http://courtinginfluence.net/nominees.php.

30. The passage is from a questionnaire available at http://courtinginfluence.net/nominees.php.

31. Data on the age of Bush appointees is from Sheldon Goldman et al., "W. Bush's Judiciary: The First Term Record," 88 *Judicature* 244 (2005).

32. Data on the Latino vote (from exit polls) is available at www.cnn.com.

33. The Hruska quote appears in Richard Harris, *The Decision* (1971), at 110.

34. Quotes from the ABA reports come from the ABA's Web site, at www.abanet.org/scfedjud/statements.html.

35. The quote about Nixon insiders considering Carswell a "boob" appears in John Massaro, *Supremely Political* (1990), at 6. The story about Truman and FDR appears in Sheldon Goldman, *Picking Federal Judges* (1997), at 21–22.

36. The quote about James Wilson and other information about the qualifications of Washington's appointees is in Henry J. Abraham, *Justice, Presidents, and Senators* (1999), at 59.

37. The quote about the FBI's role comes from a memorandum written by Warren Christopher, then a deputy attorney general in the Johnson administration and excerpted in Sheldon Goldman, *Picking Federal Judges* (1997), at 9–10.

38. The quote about Nixon and homosexuals appears in John W. Dean, *The Rehnquist Choice* (2001), at 20.

39. Until the G. H. W. Bush administration, the ABA used a four-point rating system: "exceptionally well qualified," "well qualified," "qualified," and "not qualified."

40. The quote about the ABA Committee's criteria appears on its Web site, www.abanet.org/scfedjud/home.html.

41. Data on ABA ratings of appointees are from Sheldon Goldman et al., "W. Bush's Judiciary: The First Term Record," 88 *Judicature* 244 (2005) and Sheldon Goldman, *Picking Federal Judges* (1997).

42. The story about Mildred Lillie and the ABA appears in Dean's *The Rehnquist Choice* (2001). See also Alan B. Morrison's insightful review of Dean's book, in 55 *Stanford Law Review* 1457 (2003).

43. The Clinton insider is Sarah Wilson and the quote appears in her "Appellate Judicial Appointments During the Clinton Presidency: An Inside Perspective," 5 *Journal of Appellate Practice and Process* 29 (2003).

44. On the relationship between the ABA and the Carter administration, see Mary L. Clark, "Carter's Groundbreaking Appointment of Women to the Federal Bench: His Other 'Human Rights' Record," 11 *American University Journal of Gender, Social Policy and Law* 1131 (2003). The story about Krauskopf comes from this paper.

45. The quote from Gonzales comes from the letter he wrote to the ABA and is available at www.whitehouse.gov/news/releases/2001/03/20010322-5.html.

46. For the debate over alleged bias in the ABA's ratings, see James Lindgren, "Examining the American Bar Association's Ratings of Nominees to the U.S. Courts of Appeals for Political Bias, 1989–2000," 17 *Journal of Law and Politics* 1 (2001) and Michael J. Saks and Neil Vidmar, "A Flawed Search for Bias in the American Bar Association's Ratings for Prospective Judicial Nominees: A Critique of the Lindgren Study," 17 *Journal of Law and Politics* 219 (2001).

47. Edward S. Corwin's quote appears in his *Liberty Against Government* (1948), at 138.

48. Ratings are from the ABA Committee's Web site, www.abanet.org/scfedjud/home.html.

49. The *New York Times* editorial appeared on October 25, 2003, at 18A.

50. We draw the story about Irizarry from Raymond Hernandez, "Judicial Nomination Advances," *New York Times*, October 31, 2003, at 5B.

51. President Bush has invoked the ABA's rating to shore up support for several other nominees besides Estrada, including Terrence Boyle, Priscilla Owen, and John G. Roberts. See, e.g., "President's Statement on Judicial Nominations," May 9, 2005, available at www.whitehouse.gov/news/releases/2005/05/20050509-7.html; "Remarks by the President on Judicial Confirmations," October 30, 2002, available at www.whitehouse.gov/news/releases/2002/10/20021030-6.html.

52. The story about FDR and Floyd comes from Sheldon Goldman, *Picking Federal Judges* (1997), at 27–28.

53. The quotes from Orrin Hatch appear in Neil A. Lewis, "Here Come the Judges," *New York Times,* December 1, 2002, Sec. 4, at 3; and Orrin G. Hatch, "At Last a Look at the Facts," 11 *George Mason Law Review* 467 (2003). The quote about Hatch's "aggressive" use of blue slips during the Clinton years comes from John Anthony Maltese, "Anatomy of a Confirmation Mess," *Jurist,* April 15, 2004.

54. The account of Joe Biden expressing support for a well-qualified candidate is from David Alistair Yalof, *Pursuit of Justices* (1999), 158

55. These quotations come from various sources on the White House Web site on judicial nominations, www.whitehouse.gov/infocus/judicialnominees.

56. The story of the Fletcher appointment comes from Sarah Wilson, "Appellate Judicial Appointments During the Clinton Presidency: An Inside Perspective," 5 *Journal of Appellate Practice and Process* 29 (2003).

57. The legal scholar Michael J. Gerhardt has written extensively on the importance of norms in appointments process, and the dangers presidents face when they do not follow them. See his "Norm Theory and the Future of the Federal Appointments Process," 50 *Duke Law Journal* 1687 (2001), and "Federal Judicial Selection in the New Millennium: Judicial Selection as War," 36 *U.C. Davis Law Review* 667 (2003). Our material (including the story about Bush and the FBI reports) draws on the latter work.

58. The account of the Gregory appointment comes from Sarah Wilson, "Appellate Judicial Appointments During the Clinton Presidency: An Inside Perspective," 5 *Journal of Appellate Practice and Process* 29 (2003), and Louis Fisher, "Recess Appointments of Federal Judges," September 5, 2001, Congressional Research Service, RL31112. We also draw on Fisher for data and other information on recess appointments more generally.

59. The accusations against Pickering resulted from his work as a district court judge to reduce a seven-and-a-half-year sentence in a cross-burning case to twenty-seven months, when the ringleader in the case had received a suspended sentence. Pickering thought the disparity unfair. More relevantly, Pickering risked his life by testifying against the KKK in 1966, sent his children to desegregated Mississippi public schools in the 1970s when many chose segregated private schools, desegregated his church, and had the strong support of African-American leaders in Mississippi who know him well.

60. The Daschle quote appears in Sheryl Gay Stolberg, "Democrats Issue Threat to Block Court Nominees," *New York Times*, March 27, 2004, at 1A.

61. On Bush's promise not to make any more recess appointments, see Neil A. Lewis, "Deal Ends Impasse over Judicial Nominees," *New York Times*, May 19, 2004, at 19A.

Chapter 4

1. We adapt the account of Bork's nomination from Jeffrey A. Segal and Harold J. Spaeth, *The Supreme Court and the Attitudinal Model* (2002), at 194–196.

2. Elena Kagan uses the term "lovefest" to describe the Ginsburg nomination in her article, "Confirmation Messes, Old and New," 62 *University of Chicago Law Review* 919 (1995).

3. For more on the Senate's Committee on the Judiciary, visit its Web site at http://judiciary.senate.gov. For a current perspective, see Orrin G. Hatch, "At Last a Look at the Facts: The Truth About the Judicial Selection Process," 11 *George Mason Law Review* 467 (2003).

4. For more on the importance of hearings, see Mitchel A. Sollenberger, "The Law: Must the Senate Take a Floor Vote on a Presidential Judicial Nominee?" 34 *Presidential Studies Quarterly* 420 (2004).

5. On the importance of timing, we draw on Charles R. Shipan and Megan L. Shannon, "Delaying Justice(s): A Duration Analysis of Supreme Court Confirmations," 47 *American Journal of Political Science* 654 (2003); Sarah A. Binder and Forrest Maltzman, "Senatorial Delay in Confirming Federal Judges, 1947–1998," 46 *American Journal of Political Science* 190 (2002).

6. Information on blue slips comes from Betsy Palmer, "Evolution of the Senate's Role in the Nomination and Confirmation Process," Congressional Research Service, RL31948, June 5, 2003, and Sheldon Goldman, "The Senate and Judicial Nominations," *Extensions,* spring 2004, at 4. Information about Hatch's use of blue slips during the Clinton years comes from John Anthony Maltese, "Anatomy of a Confirmation Mess," *Jurist,* April 15, 2004; the emphasis is ours. Leahy's comments about Judiciary Committee proce-

dures under Hatch appear in "Statement of Patrick Leahy, April 1, 2003," available at http://judiciary.senate.gov/member_statement.cfm?id=682andwit_id=50.

7. The story about Ted Stewart comes from Michael J. Gerhardt, "Judicial Selection as War," 36 *U.C. Davis Law Review Rev.* 667 (2003), at 682.

8. The quote from Krogh comes from David Alistair Yalof, *Pursuit of Justices* (1997), at 115; the quote from *Harper's Weekly* is taken from James W. Ely, *The Chief Justiceship of Melville W. Fuller, 1888–1910* (1995), at 23.

9. For studies of delay on the federal courts, see Charles R. Shipan and Megan L. Shannon, "Delaying Justice(s): A Duration Analysis of Supreme Court Confirmations," 47 *American Journal of Political Science* 654 (2003); Sarah A. Binder and Forrest Maltzman, "Senatorial Delay in Confirming Federal Judges, 1947–1998," 46 *American Journal of Political Science* 190 (2002).

10. Figures on the number of "controversial" lower court nominations vary slightly from study to study, as do data on interest group participation in lower court proceedings. We draw on Roy B. Flemming et al., "Witnesses at the Confirmations? The Appearance of Organized Interests at Senate Hearings of Federal Judicial Appointments, 1945–1992," 51 *Political Research Quarterly* 617 (1998); Amy Steigerwalt, "The Four Tracks to Confirmation," paper presented at the 2004 annual meeting of the Midwest Political Science Association, Chicago, IL; Lauren C. Bell, "Senate Confirmations in an Interest Group Age," *Extensions,* spring 2004.

11. The quote from Davis about press coverage and other information in this paragraph is from Richard Davis, *Electing Justice* (2005), at 24.

12. Data on the number of articles about Ginsburg are from Richard Davis, *Electing Justice* (2005), at 98.

13. The editorial on Ginsburg is "A Touch of Class for the Court," *New York Times,* July 25, 1993, 16 (Sect. 4).

14. The editorial on Thomas is "Against Clarence Thomas; Even 'Don't Know' Calls for a 'No' Vote," *New York Times,* October 15, 1991, 24A.

15. We draw the story about Matthews from Scott Ainsworth and John Anthony Maltese, "National Grange Influence on the Supreme Court Confirmation of Stanley Matthews," 20 *Social Science History* 45 (1996).

16. The Ehrlichman quote appears in John Massaro, *Supremely Political* (1990), at 22.

17. For more on the interest group campaign for and against Bork, see Gregory A. Caldeira and John R, Wright, "Lobbying for Justice: Organized Interests, Supreme Court Nominations, and the United States Senate," 42 *American Journal of Political Science* 499 (1998). The quote about the "extraordinary effort" mounted by groups against Bork comes from this article, at 509.

18. Nancy Scherer provides a glimpse into why groups participate in some lower court confirmation proceedings. See her "The Judicial Confirmation Process: Mobilizing Elites, Mobilizing Masses," 86 *Judicature* 240 (2003).

19. The quotation is from Ginsburg's testimony at her confirmation proceedings.

20. On the reaction of the White House to the vote on Bork, see Steven V. Roberts, "9–5 Panel Vote Against Bork Sends Nomination to Senate Amid Predications of Defeat," *New York Times,* October 7, 1987, at A1.

21. Information on holds comes from Amy Steigerwalt, "The Four Tracks to Confirmation," paper presented at the 2004 annual meeting of the Midwest Political Science Association, Chicago, IL; Jason M. Roberts, "Parties, Presidents, and Procedures: The Battle over Judicial Nominations in the U.S. Senate," *Extensions,* spring 2004.

22. The story about Tyler's nomination of King is taken from Lee Epstein et al., *The Supreme Court Compendium* (2003), at 364.

23. For the classic statement of members of Congress as "single-minded seekers of reelection," see David R. Mayhew, *Congress: The Electoral Connection* (1974, 2005).

24. On public opinion and the filibuster, we rely on a March 2005 sruvey by Princeton Survey Research Associates International/Newsweek, which asked a sample of Americans the following question. "U.S. (United States) Senate rules allow 41 Senators to mount a filibuster—refusing to end debate and agree to vote—to block judicial nominees. In the past, this tactic has been used by both Democrats and Republicans to prevent certain judicial nominees from being confirmed. Senate Republican leaders, whose party is now in the majority, want to take away this tactic by changing the rules to require only 51 votes, instead of 60, to break a filibuster. Would you approve or disapprove of changing Senate rules to take away the filibuster and allow all of George W. Bush's judicial nominees to get voted on by the Senate?" Of the respondents, 32 percent approved, 57 percent disapproved, and 11 percent had no opinion.

25. The quote from Hoover appears in Richard Davis, *Electing Justice* (2005), at 30.

26. When asked in May 1994 whether "the Senate should or should not confirm [Stephen G.] Breyer's nomination to the Supreme Court," only 10 percent said no. When asked "Generally speaking, do you think [Stephen G.] Breyer is qualified to be a Supreme Court justice, or is that something you don't have an opinion on?" 35 percent said yes, 4 said no, and 61 percent had no opinion. Both are ABC News/*Washington Post* polls.

27. Martin Shapiro, in "Interest Groups and Supreme Court Appointments," 84 *Northwestern University Law Review* 935 (1990), at 935, makes the claim that groups "play a small role."

28. The quote from NOW, about the electoral threat posed by interest groups, appears in Lauren C. Bell, "Senate Confirmations in an Interest Group Age," *Extensions,* spring 2004, at 22.

29. The quotes about "key votes" come from Lauren C. Bell, "Senate Confirmations in an Interest Group Age," *Extensions,* spring 2004, at 22.

30. The vote tallies are as follows:

Nominee	Votes in Favor	Votes Opposed
Earl Warren (CJ)	Voice vote	
John M. Harlan	71	11
William J. Brennan Jr.	Voice vote	
Charles E. Whittaker	96	0

Potter Stewart	71	17
Byron White	Voice vote	
Arthur J. Goldberg	Voice vote	
Abe Fortas	Voice vote	
Thurgood Marshall	69	11
Abe Fortas (CJ)*	43	44
Warren E. Burger (CJ)	74	3
Clement Haynsworth Jr.	45	55
G. Harrold Carswell	45	51
Harry A. Blackmun	94	0
Lewis F. Powell Jr.	89	1
William H. Rehnquist	68	26
John Paul Stevens	98	0
Sandra Day O'Connor	99	0
William H. Rehnquist (CJ)	65	33
Antonin Scalia	98	0
Robert H. Bork	42	58
Anthony Kennedy	97	0
David Souter	90	9
Clarence Thomas	52	48
Ruth Bader Ginsburg	96	3
Stephen G. Breyer	87	9

CJ = nominated for chief justice

*The vote on Fortas for the chief justice position was on cloture and failed to receive the necessary two-thirds vote.

Our claim about the effect of qualifications on Senate votes comes from the analysis in the text, as well as from our other work on Senate voting on Supreme Court nominees. See, e.g., Jeffrey A. Segal and Harold J. Spaeth, *The Supreme Court and the Attitudinal Model Revisited* (2002); Lee Epstein, Jeffrey A. Segal, and Nancy Staudt, "The Role of Qualifications in the Confirmation of Nominees to the U.S. Supreme Court," 32 *Florida State University Law Review* (2005); WERL, "On Tournaments for Appointing Great Justices to the U.S. Supreme Court," 78 *Southern California Law Review* 157 (2005); and Lee Epstein, René Lindstädt, Jeffrey A. Segal, and Chad Westerland, "Borked! The New Politics of Senate Voting on Supreme Court Nominees," working paper, Washington University in St. Louis, available at http://epstein.wustl.edu/research/Bork.html. What the analyses in these papers show is that ideology (specifically, the ideological distance between a senator and a nominee) and the nominee's qualifications are statistically significant explanations of senators' votes even after we control for other relevant factors (such as whether the president's party controls the Senate).

31. Segal and his colleagues introduced their method for assessing nominees' qualifications in Charles D. Cameron, Albert D. Cover, & Jeffrey A. Segal, "Senate Voting on Supreme Court Nominees: A Neo-Institutional Model," 84 *American Political Science Review* 525 (1990). Segal later updated the scores to include the four nominees subsequent to Anthony Kennedy. One

scholar critical of the approach (see Figure 4.3) is Mark Silverstein, *Judicious Choices* (1994), at 5. We decided not to use the ratings issued by the American Bar Association's Standing Committee on Federal Judiciary, even though they are (presumably) extrinsic to individual senators and are, according to the ABA, "impartial evaluations of the integrity, professional competence and judicial temperament" that "do not consider a nominee's philosophy or ideology," because they are problematic in any number of ways. One is that the committee's rating system has fluctuated with time, and even within particular periods it has lacked consistency. For example, until 1970 it typically rated a candidate as simply "qualified" or not—but not always; in 1963, it deemed Arthur Goldberg "highly acceptable" and thought it inappropriate to proffer "an opinion to the degree of qualification." Also a problem for our purposes are allegations, as we mentioned in Chapter 3, that ABA ratings evince a (liberal) ideological bias. Abraham, 22–28; for the language the ABA has used in its ratings, see Epstein et al., 359–360.

32. Here we use our qualifications scores (see Figure 4.3). The cut points are as follows: highly qualified = 0.80 to 1, qualified = 0.79 to 0, not qualified = 0 to -1.

33. The Binder and Maltzman study is Sarah A. Binder and Forrest Maltzman, "Senatorial Delay in Confirming Federal Judges, 1947–1998," 46 *American Journal of Political Science* 190 (2002).

34. The quote about the Ninth Circuit appears in Sarah A. Binder and Forrest Maltzman, "Senatorial Delay in Confirming Federal Judges, 1947–1998," 46 *American Journal of Political Science* 190 (2002).

35. Segal and his colleagues introduced their method for assessing nominees' and senators' ideologies in Charles D. Cameron, Albert D. Cover, and Jeffrey A. Segal, "Senate Voting on Supreme Court Nominees: A Neo-Institutional Model," 84 *American Political Science Review* 525 (1990). Information about the ADA scores is available on the ADA's Web site, www.adaction.org.

36. The quote comparing Janice Brown to Scalia and Thomas appears on the Web site of People for the American Way, www.pfaw.org. The NOW quote can be found at www.now.org/issues/legislat/nominees/060305-TruthBrown.html.

37. Another obstacle to the analysis of votes over lower court nominations is the lack (until recently) of recorded roll call votes. Accordingly, scholars have studied instead senators' attempts to delay nominations. See, e.g., Sarah A. Binder and Forrest Maltzman, "Senatorial Delay in Confirming Federal Judges, 1947–1998," 46 *American Journal of Political Science* 190 (2002).

38. Four days after her nomination, on June 18, 1993, Gallup asked: "Ruth Bader Ginsburg is a federal judge who has been nominated by President [Bill] Clinton to serve on the United States Supreme Court. Would you like to see the Senate vote in favor of Ginsburg serving on the Supreme Court, or not?" Of the responses, 53 percent were favorable; 14 percent were unfavorable; 33 had no opinion. By the time of her confirmation in Au-

gust, 67 percent approved of her appointment, 21 disapproved, and 12 had no opinion.

By contrast, around the time of the Senate's vote on Bork, 51 percent of Gallup's survey respondents said Bork should not be confirmed, 32 percent said he should be, and 17 percent had no opinion.

Chapter 5

1. The phrase "puzzling and relatively ad hoc" appears in Cass R. Sunstein, "Law and Administration After *Chevron*," 90 *Columbia Law Review* 2071 (1990), at 2082.

2. The whistleblowing discussion follows Frank B. Cross and Emerson H. Tiller, "Judicial Partisanship and Obedience to Legal Doctrine: Whistleblowing on the Federal Courts of Appeals," 107 *Yale Law Journal* 2155 (1998); Harry Edwards, "Collegiality and Decision Making on the D.C. Circuit," *Virginia Law Review* 1335 (1998); and Patricia M. Wald, "A Response to Tiller and Cross," 99 *Columbia Law Review* 235 (1999).

3. Nixon's remark about the Supreme Court appears in "Transcript of President's Announcements," *New York Times,* October 22, 1971, at 24.

4. We derived the figures on active lower court judges appointed by Johnson, Nixon, Carter, and Reagan from the Federal Judicial Center's Federal Judges Biographical Database, available at www.fjc.gov/public/home.nsf/hisj.

5. The presidential and scholarly quotes on presidential success are drawn from Jeffrey A. Segal, Richard J. Timpone, and Robert M. Howard, "Buyer Beware? Presidential Success through Supreme Court Appointments," 53 *Political Research Quarterly* (2000), at 559, and Lawrence Tribe, *God Save This Honorable Court* (1985), at 60. See also Donald E. Lively, "The Supreme Court Appointment Process: In Search of Constitutional Roles and Responsibilities," 59 *Southern California Law Review* 551 (1986).

6. To determine the president's ideology, we rely on Keith Poole's work, which in turn assesses ideology by analyzing the president's positions over bills before Congress. See, e.g., Nolan N. McCarty and Keith T. Poole, "Veto Power and Legislation: An Empirical Analysis of Executive and Legislative Bargaining from 1961–1986," 11 *Journal of Law, Economics, and Organization* 282 (1995). While presidents do not cast roll call votes in Congress, on most important pieces of legislation the president announces a "vote intention"—that is, how he would vote on the bill if afforded the opportunity. Since the early 1950s *Congressional Quarterly* has published these presidential vote intentions. If, for example, the president announced his intention to vote in favor of a bill curtailing abortion rights, that would be a conservative "vote"; if he opposed such a bill, that would be a liberal "vote."

7. We can summarize the relationship depicted in Figure 5.1 through a simple statistic, called the correlation coefficient, or r—such that an r of $+1$ would mean a perfectly positive relationship between a president's ideology and a nominee's; in other words, knowledge of a president's ideology would enable us to predict perfectly the ideology of his nominees (and in the "right"

direction). In this case, the *r* is +.64, suggesting a reasonably strong relationship: the more liberal (or conservative) the president, the more liberal (or conservative) the nominee.

8. For more on the partisan goals of presidents when appointing appeals court judges, see Sheldon Goldman, *Picking Federal Judges* (1997). The Tenth Circuit case we discuss is the text is *Adarand Constructors, Inc. v. Pena* (1994); the Supreme Court vacated and remanded the Tenth's judgment in 1995. Finally, in a forthcoming book, *Scoring Points: Politicians, Activists and the Lower Court Appointment Process*, Nancy Scherer argues that in the 1960s Kennedy and later Johnson moved away from senatorial courtesy to prevent southern Democrats from naming segregationists to the bench. Hence, on her account, the ideology of judges appointed during this period (and perhaps thereafter) may be closer to the appointing president than to home-state senators. Nonetheless, she also suggests that even if "senators do not choose appellate judges anymore," the party "elites in a particular state from which the president selects his appellate judges" may still play an important role.

9. Data on the number of Democrats appointed by George W. Bush are from Sheldon Goldman et al., "W. Bush's Judiciary: The First Term Record," 88 *Judicature* 244 (2005)

10. Information on the difference between the president's ideology and the ideology of the median member of the Senate of his party are from Keith Poole's (first dimension) Common Space scores, available at http://voteview.com/readmeb.htm (file last updated March 9, 2005). Kohl was the median Democrat (or shared that position) in the Senate during all but two of the Clinton years (1997–98), when the median was Senator Ron Wyden of Oregon).

11. For more on the public's reaction to *Bush v. Gore,* see James L. Gibson, Gregory A. Caldeira, and Lester Kenyatta Spence, "The Supreme Court and the US Presidential Election of 2000," 33 *British Journal of Political Science* 535 (2003). See also Howard Gillman's excellent book, *The Votes That Counted* (2001).

12. Data on voting patterns in the U.S. Courts of Appeals are from Cass Sunstein, David Schkade, and Lisa Ellman, "Ideological Voting on Federal Courts of Appeals: A Preliminary Investigation," 90 *Virginia Law Review* 301 (2004).

13. The quotes about convictions being impervious to panel effects appear in Cass Sunstein, David Schkade, and Lisa Ellman, "Ideological Voting on Federal Courts of Appeals: A Preliminary Investigation," 90 *Virginia Law Review* 301 (2004), at 335.

15. Data on environmental cases are from Cass Sunstein, David Schkade, and Lisa Ellman, "Ideological Voting on Federal Courts of Appeals: A Preliminary Investigation," 90 *Virginia Law Review* 301 (2004).

16. Brian J. Moraski and Charles R. Shipan, "The Politics of Supreme Court Nominations," 43 *American Journal of Political Science* 1069 (1999), detail the extent to which presidents must consider the preferences of the Senate when they make their judicial appointments. They show that most presidents have not been particularly constrained. Exceptions include Truman

(Clark, Minton, and Harlan), Johnson (both Fortas nominations), and George H. W. Bush (Souter and Thomas).

17. The correlation between presidential ideology and the judicial voting (see Figure 5.4) is +.64.

18. The correlation between voting of the (mean) appellate court judge and the ideology of his or her appointing president is .99. Data here and to follow on circuit court voting are from Donald R. Songer's U.S. Court of Appeals Database, available at www.as.uky.edu/polisci/ulmerproject/databases.htm

19. The figure depicts judges' decisions in civil liberties case (criminal procedure, First Amendment, civil rights, due process, and privacy), with liberal votes favoring the accused in criminal cases, and those asserting the broadest First Amendment, due process, privacy, and civil rights claim (with the exception of affirmative action cases). The results we show are for a sample of circuit court judges (those who voted in twenty or more cases), whether appointed under senatorial courtesy or not.

20. William E. Kovacic, "Reagan's Judicial Appointees and Antitrust in the 1990s," 60 *Fordham Law Review* 49 (1991). The quote appears on page 89.

21. The following figures demonstrate the relationship between presidential ideology and the votes of circuit court judges when senatorial courtesy was and was not in effect:

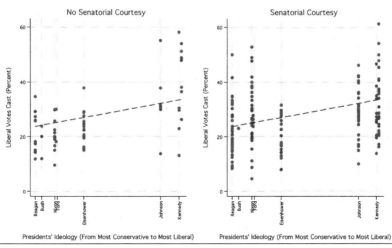

Each point represents a judge. The dotted line represents a prediction of the judge's votes based on the ideology of the appointing president. The closer a point to the line, the stronger the association between the president's ideology and his judge's votes. Judges above the line more liberally than predicted; judges below the line vote more conservatively than predicted.

The correlation between presidential ideology and the votes of circuit court judges when senatorial courtesy was in effect is +.23; it jumps to +.49 when senatorial courtesy was not in effect.

On the limited nature of the relationship between presidential ideology and judges' decisions in courtesy situations, see Micheal Giles, Virginia Hettinger, and Todd Peppers, "Picking Federal Judges: A Note on Policy and Partisan Selection Agendas," 54 *Political Research Quarterly* 623 (2001). We thank the authors for providing us with their data on courtesy appointments.

We ought to note that while senatorial courtesy limits the impact of presidential ideology, partisan control of the Senate does not. At least according to the political scientist Nancy Scherer, appointment during divided government appears to have little impact on the decisions of appeals court judges. She found no differences in the votes cast by Reagan judges appointed before or after Democrats regained control of the Senate in 1987, nor did she find differences in the decisional propensities of Clinton judges appointed before or after Republicans took control of the Senate in 1995. See Nancy Scherer, "Who Drives the Ideological Makeup of the Lower Federal Courts in a Divided Government?" 35 *Law and Society Review* 191–218 (2001).

22. The Friedman quote appears in Richard Friedman, "Tribal Myths: Ideology and the Confirmation of Supreme Court Nominations," 95 *Yale Law Journal* 1283 (1986), at 1291.

23. The comparison between Presidents Nixon and Reagan in terms of their relative success in moving the Court draws from Jeffrey A. Segal and Robert Howard, "Justices and Presidents," in Steven A. Shull, ed., *Presidential Policymaking* (1999), at 172–176, and Jeffrey A. Segal and Harold J. Spaeth, *The Supreme Court and the Attitudinal Model Revisited* (2002), at 217–222. Reagan's quote appears in the *New York Times*, October 9, 1986, at A32.

24. For data on presidents' (including Clinton's) success in shifting the ideological composition of the circuits, see Lee Epstein, Andrew D. Martin, Jeffrey A. Segal, and Chad Westerland, "The Judicial Common Space," paper delivered at Northwestern Law School's Conference on Law and Positive Political Theory, 2005, available at http://epstein.wustl.edu/research/JCS.html.

25. William H. Rehnquist, *The Supreme Court: How It Was, How It Is* (1987), at 236.

Chapter 6

1. The quote from Bork appears in his *The Tempting of America* (1990), at 348.

Index

Page numbers in *italics* refer to illustrations or figures.